Joe Rogaly was born in Johannesburg, South Africa, in 1935; he has always worked for newspapers, except for a few spells out of the trade when he has been dish clearer, tea boy, and invoice clerk. Starting as an apprentice in the printing works of the *Rand Daily Mail*, during which time he was a member of the typographical union, he went on to read English, politics and economics at the University of the Witwatersrand. After a few years as reporter on the *Rand Daily Mail* he came to settle permanently in England in 1959. He joined the National Union of Journalists, and remains a member. Until 1965, he wrote for the *Economist*, specializing in African affairs. He joined the *Financial Times* in that year, and was Washington correspondent from 1967 to 1969. Since then, he has written a weekly commentary, 'Society Today', for the *Financial Times*, where he is now an assistant editor. This is his second book; the first was *Parliament for the People*, a handbook of electoral reform, published in 1976.

Joe Rogaly

Grunwick

Penguin Books

Penguin Books Ltd, Harmondsworth,
Middlesex, England
Penguin Books, 625 Madison Avenue,
New York, New York 10022, U.S.A.
Penguin Books Australia Ltd, Ringwood,
Victoria, Australia
Penguin Books Canada Ltd, 2801 John Street,
Markham, Ontario, Canada L3R 1B4
Penguin Books (N.Z.) Ltd, 182–190 Wairau Road,
Auckland 10, New Zealand

First published 1977
Copyright © Joe Rogaly, 1977
All rights reserved

Made and printed in Great Britain by
Cox & Wyman Ltd, London, Reading and Fakenham
Set in Intertype Times

Acknowledgements

It would not have been possible to write this
book at such speed or to include as much
information without the invaluable assistance
of Mrs Kay Blair, of the *Financial Times*
Library.

Several people have been kind enough to read
parts of the text and make helpful suggestions,
including: Jim Jump, Roy Grantham, John
Gorst, MP, Jack Dromey, Geoffrey Bindman,
and Barbara Smith. The contents of the book
are all my own responsibility.

For permission to quote from the Scarman
report, *Report of a Court of Inquiry . . . into a
dispute between Grunwick . . . and APEX*, Cmnd
6922, Crown copyright, acknowledgement is
made to Her Majesty's Stationery Office.

J.R.
September 1977

Contents

1 The walk-out: August 1976

It had been the hottest, driest summer that London could re-
member. The meteorologists said that there had not been such a
rain-free August since 1949, or such a sunny one since 1947.
Average temperatures were around 75°F, but there were times
when they hit the eighties. This may not mean much in Arizona,
or Tanzania, but when it happened in London, day after day,
people did not know what to make of it. Strange things occurred. An Arab family bought a house near Highgate and,
thinking that temperatures in England were not so low as they
had been led to expect when they left Saudi Arabia, insisted on
having full air-conditioning installed.

In the parks, and on Hampstead Heath, people swam and
took happy snapshots of one another as if they were by the
seaside. At one swimming pool, on the south side of the Heath,
the crowds were so thick, and the horseplay among the young
men was so uncontrolled, that a boy was murdered, drowned
while being held under water.

Not far away, in Brent, business at Grunwick Processing
Laboratories was booming. Most of their work is done in the
summer, when the holiday film comes into be developed and
printed. It is like the ice-cream trade: sunny days create so
much demand that those who work in it must move twice as
fast as usual simply to keep in step. In the mail-order room of
Grunwick the piles of photographs kept coming in and out. It is
a long, brightly painted room, with no windows opening directly to the outside, but with air-conditioning to make up for it.

Sadly, the air-conditioning machinery was out of order
during most of that August. The workers sat in rows at long
tables, their busy fingers sorting the negatives, and prints, and
payment slips, for crediting to accounts or posting back to the

9

customers. There were about a hundred of them, mostly Asians from East Africa, people who had been driven out of Uganda by President Amin, or who had come with less fanfare following the more discreet and less uncivilized pressure exercised by the African governments of Kenya and Tanzania.

Back home, work in a high temperature was normal: most of them had been shopkeepers, or office workers. But as all visitors to East Africa will know, the people adjust to the heat out there in one of two ways. Either they work in shirt-sleeves in modern buildings with air conditioning or, more often, they move at a pace that is suitable to the clinging atmosphere, an atmosphere that sometimes gives the visitor the sensation of wading through warm water. At Grunwick that August the photographs kept coming in and the English climate was turning East African, but there was neither air conditioning nor an East African pace to make the day more bearable.

What happened on that particular afternoon at first seemed insignificant; just a little squabble of an everyday kind, in a busy factory at a time when tempers were naturally high. Yet it was the start of a remarkable political – industrial struggle, in which all the worst instincts that mar the British polity were revealed. Few of the subsequently famous protagonists came well out of the Grunwick affair, which is perhaps natural in a series of events that is best described as farce. Only the largely unknown Asian workers themselves, on both sides of the picket lines that were soon formed, avoided the absurdities and emotional posturing of those who made the national headlines. But because of those absurdities the inadequacy of English industrial law was made manifest and the class conflict, which is at the heart of the British disease, was given new, and at times ugly, force. None of this would have been foreseen when the first pebble began to slip on that hot day in August 1976.

Perhaps the heat contributed to the sense of grievance felt by some of the workers. One of them, Devshi Bhudia, who was just over nineteen years old, talked with young friends about joining a trade union. One of those friends was Sunil Desai, a student who, like his mother, was at work in the mail-order department. What they said to one another at the time is not recorded; later, after all the trouble had begun, the main allegations were that wages were low, working conditions were poor, overtime was compulsory, holidays were short and restricted to the winter months, the management was overbearing, and unfair sackings were common. Above all, there seemed to be no way of settling these issues; what was needed, the boys decided, was a union.

Even if he had overheard the talk among his young employees Mr Malcolm Alden, the supervisor of the mail-order department, would not have understood it. Mr Alden, thirty-three, a short, pale Englishman whose later statements indicated a strong concern for maintaining a disciplined workforce, sat in a small glass box at one end of the mail-order room. He controlled everything with meticulous efficiency, noting who was late, and who was absent, who was a good worker and who seemed to be slacking. He could not, however, speak or understand Gujerati, the native language of most of the Asians he watched through his glass window-pane.

Thus it must have come as a complete surprise when about a week after the boys had discussed trade unions among themselves a few of them began to demonstrate their sense of grievance in a suitably melodramatic manner. The evidence given to the subsequent Court of Inquiry under Lord Justice Scarman conflicts on some points of detail about the size of the task given by Mr Alden to Devshi Bhudia and the boys working with him that day, but their response can be deduced from the following exchange between one of them, Chandrakant Patel, a student, and Mr Mervyn Heald, QC for Grunwick:

Heald: 'You then worked very slowly?'

Patel: 'We worked slowly, yes.'

'As a protest?'

'As a protest, yes.'

'And, indeed, more than a protest, as a provocation to Mr Alden because he could see you?'

'Well, we slowed down because he pressurized us . . .'

'He could see that you were working slowly from where he was?'

'He might be, yes, because I was facing on the other side so I could not help probably seeing him.'

11

The point could hardly have been missed. This was the early afternoon of 20 August 1976, a day the London Weather Centre records as 75°F and sunny. It was the peak of the season for Grunwick and, being a Friday, one of the busiest days of the week. Photographs not sent back to customers by that night would only add to the congestion the following week. The tone of Mr Alden's response to the go-slow is not verifiable from the several accounts given, but he has been described by a number of people, both inside the Court of Inquiry and out, as one who might lose his temper in such circumstances, and, indeed, even the calmest of supervisors might have felt sorely tried.

Devshi Bhudia, who said he was being paid £29 for thirty-five hours' work, told the Court of Inquiry that he had found himself another job at £41 a week, and that he informed Mr Alden of this when called into the office to explain the go-slow. Mr Alden says he did not. Their accounts differ on several such details, but curiously the point at which they agree is where the young man says of his working relationship with Mr Alden, 'actually, he was all right with me' and his former supervisor says of him, 'I never had any real complaints about him.' If the quarrel started between these two its subsequent development cannot be explained by their earlier relationship at work.

Anyhow, Devshi was sacked, and he walked out through the factory gates. There is a dispute about whether he signalled the others as he did so, but it does not seem to matter. Three of them went into Mr Alden's glass cage and Chandrakant Patel said that he too would leave. Out they went, the four of them, Devshi included, and hung about just beyond the gates.

But this did not end the troubles of Mr Alden. A scene that was to achieve far greater fame was yet to come. The picture through his glass pane that afternoon might have made a suitable cover for a Sunday magazine article on industrial relations in India. The people sitting in long rows, bent over their sorting and their folding were not only students, but also older women, some of them the mothers of students working for Grunwick. They sat on their saris, faces set, as the sound of Capital Radio blared forth, piped in by the company because in earlier days people had brought their own tape recorders and radios and,

12

Mr Alden told the inquiry, 'you would have English music and six feet away Oriental music'.

About half-way down the sorting-room, sitting at a table that left her with her back to Mr Alden, was Mrs Jayaben Desai, a short middle-aged Indian lady, who is so well able to look after herself in any verbal exchange that at the Inquiry Lord Justice Scarman told her in the midst of a long cross-examination by Mr Heald:

'You are absolutely right to insist on questions being put with particularity by counsel, and so far in two skirmishes you have emerged the victor.'

Mrs Desai has, of course, done more than that. To all who took up the cause of the Grunwick workers and many others she has become a symbol of their cause. Her image is that of the small but determined figure in the posters, the motherly picket surrounded by policemen, the champion of trade union rights. From this point of view she could acquire as important a place in the British social consciousness as Eliza, tripping across the ice-floes to save her life in *Uncle Tom's Cabin*, did for nine-teenth-century Americans.

The way Mrs Desai tells it, she was preparing to leave that evening (she says at five to seven, the company says around six since they have a clocking-in card of hers marked 6.15) when 'one of the foremen came behind and asked me "Mrs Desai, who told you to pack up?" Then,' she told the Inquiry, 'I say "Why do you ask me when you have never asked me before?" ' This led to a considerable row, whose nature differs according to which of the participants is describing it. Mrs Desai's version is that she was called into the office and shouted at; Mr Alden's, that he had left his office to walk down to where Mrs Desai was sitting, that he found her in heated argument with Mr Peter Diffy, his under-manager, and that he had some difficulty per-suading her to come into the office to discuss the matter calmly.

This is how Mrs Desai put it at the Inquiry, held in a base-ment of the Piccadilly Hotel, ten months later.

'I say, "Look, Mr Alden, why you bring me in the office? I am here to explain something and I want to know what is going on. If you want to shout at me I am not prepared to listen to what you are talking about. If you are prepared to listen to me I am prepared to listen to you as well, but if you shout like that to me I am not talking to you."

'Then he started to threaten me and warn me; he said, "Look, Mrs Desai, I warn you." I know that they are the tactics they always use; they give a warning the first time and they sack you, because they do not have any evidence as to why they have sacked you.

'As soon as I heard that "I warn you", I stopped him in the middle and said, "Look, I do not want to work with you; I do not want your warning. I respect you all the time and expect the same respect from you, and in this condition I am not prepared to work with you. Please give me my cards straight away. I am leaving." '

And this is Mr Alden's version; given at the same Inquiry:

'She was obviously a little excited but she was constantly interrupting me and I must admit I did not find it terribly easy to understand what she was saying, but she did interrupt me and I could not finish a single sentence without getting some interruption. This was all, just a few seconds, but the impression I have all these months later is that I could not simply finish one sentence without her interrupting.'

Asked by his counsel, Mr Heald, 'Then did the subject seem to change after a little bit?' Mr Alden went on:

'All of a sudden she kind of exploded and said: "I want my freedom. I am going. I have had enough." '

'When you say she exploded, what effect did that have on the tone of voice she was using?'

'She shouted. She shouted very loudly.'

'Thereafter did she leave Mr Diffy's office and go into . . .'

'She immediately stormed out of Mr Diffy's office and Mr Diffy followed her out and we trailed down the office behind whilst she was shouting.'

'What language was she shouting in?'

'At that stage it was a mixture of Gujerati and English. She was obviously lapsing into Gujerati but also shouting some phrases in English.'

'Could you understand what she was shouting about?'

' "I want my freedom" is the phrase that stands out in my mind as being the one that she used a number of times.'

People hearing this on that Tuesday of the Inquiry, which had moved from the Piccadilly Hotel to the new Government Press Centre in Little St James's Street, could not but refer back to Mrs Desai's evidence of the previous Monday. When she came out of Mr Diffy's office, she had said,

'I addressed everybody, "Look, my friends, this thing happened to me, and it could happen to you tomorrow. You have to understand what is the treatment you are getting from these people. I am asking this in front of Mr Alden and I am asking him why he is not employing any white girls in this department." Mr Diffy was standing there and I was asking them, "Look we are hard-working people and we are working with loyalty and these people are taking advantage of us. We have small money and they are taking hard work from us – standing on our backs all the time and taking work by forcing us with a small amount of money . . . do not understand he sacked me. That is why I am asking you in front of him, "Please give me my cards." '

The evidence from Mr Diffy, who was described by some of the strikers as easier to approach than Mr Alden, was that Mrs Desai's son, Sunil, who was working there for the second or third year running as a student, joined his mother in the shouting until they both left.

Had that scene been premeditated? No, said the Scarman report, after the Inquiry a year later. In the long run it does not affect the issue much if it had, because the important point is that the Desais clearly felt aggrieved about Grunwick. But there is no doubt that the idea of joining a trade union was in Mrs Desai's mind before that hot Friday.

Asked by Mr Stuart Shields, QC, counsel for the trade union APEX, how she came to think of a union, she informed the Inquiry:

'I told you before my husband is working with the Rank Organization and obviously on the dining table we are talking sometimes about my job and his job. I was explaining everything that happens in my job and he was explaining – an exchange of ideas. He once told me: "In your place if there is a union this type of management cannot behave like this towards you." '

From his table at the head of the Court of Inquiry, seated with his two lay assessors, Mr Pat Lowry, Director of Personnel at British Leyland, and Mr Terry Parry, General Secretary of the Fire Brigades Union, Lord Justice Scarman commented that Mrs Desai's description of family conferences and talking about jobs seemed very reasonable and human.

When she and her son walked out that Friday evening they found Devshi and the others standing outside the gates. The then personnel manager of Grunwick, a Mr Stacey, was talking to them. She told the Inquiry that he had said, ' "Look, if you have any grievances you should come to me. Why you walk out?" . . . I reached there and I said, "What is he doing here?" ' And later in her evidence she added that she had told the boys, 'It is a problem for always for everybody. Nobody knows when they will get sacked. Why don't we form a union in this company so we can get our jobs secure and good conditions and good behaviour from the management.'

On 12 July 1977, the following session of the Inquiry, she was being cross-examined once again about her reasons for wanting a union. Lord Justice Scarman:

'What you are saying is if you have someone to speak for you and someone on your side who is independent then you have a greater sense of security?'

'Yes, and that is what we want.'

'It might interest you to know, Mrs Desai, that is the origin of the legal profession.'

So it was that by the end of that Friday Mr Alden had lost six of his workers. According to Devshi Bhudia they spent most of the weekend talking about what to do next. The upshot was a decision to get a list of signatures, to build support for their plan to join a union. On the Monday morning, 23 August, they stood outside the factory gate with rudimentary placards, one of which read 'Grunwicks is a Zoo'. As fellow-workers from the mail-order department came out of Dollis Hill underground station and turned right to walk the few yards to the factory gate they asked them to sign their names; in the later evidence there was disagreement between Grunwick and the strikers as to what people were told they were signing for. To the outsider it seems likely that at least some of them knew the answer very well, since the Asians in the mail-order department mostly belonged to a fairly close-knit community, and news of a kind had presumably travelled among them over the weekend.

It was plain that the would-be trade unionists needed advice. Sunil Desai went on his bicycle to the Citizens' Advice Bureau, where he was given the telephone numbers of the TUC and the Brent Trades Council. By some quirk of fate he was advised when making these calls that APEX, originally a union of clerks and now an umbrella union for various kinds of white-collar workers, would be appropriate. (Whether other, similar, unions would have taken up their case in quite the way that APEX later did is uncertain; some might have said that it is not customary for unions to take on people already in dispute, just as individuals who are injured in a factory and then suddenly apply to become union members so that their workmen's compensation can be fought for by professionals might be told: 'you should have joined sooner.')

When Sunil eventually got through to Mr Len Gristey, the London organizer of APEX, it turned out that a local branch meeting of the union was due the following night. Mr Gristey, a friendly, old-school trade unionist said that he would see everyone from Grunwick after that meeting. This was the first contact with APEX, so far as is known, and, indeed it was not until the Tuesday night, 24 August 1976, that the initial sixty or so Grunwick workers completed their membership forms and were officially enrolled.

But before that happened on the Monday, there was another shock in store for Mr Alden. He later described it in his evidence to the Inquiry. He had noticed the half-dozen pickets on his way into work, but it was not until after lunch, at about 2.30, that Mr Diffy told him that he had heard that the staff was being asked to walk out at three o'clock.

Heald: 'Then at three o'clock did a number of mail-order staff get up from where they were working and walk out?'

Alden: 'Yes.'

'Did you speak to any of them?'

'Yes.'

'Asking them what they were doing?'

'Yes. I knew this was some form of walk-out but I must admit I was staggered at the numbers and the individuals themselves that were walking out . . .'

He heard that this substantial section of his workforce was going off to another Grunwick plant, round the block at Cobbold Road. A director of the company, thirty-nine-year-old John Hickey, raced ahead in his car to warn the management there. The gates were closed as the strikers arrived. Asked at the Inquiry what happened then, Mr Hickey replied: 'They lost complete control of themselves. There was an awful lot of shouting . . . as we are adjoining an engineering works, there are lots of metal and bars and things like this outside the premises. Some of the crowd had got hold of these and ran down between the two production buildings banging on the windows . . . a considerable number of windows was smashed or cracked.'

Devshi Bhudia was also there. His evidence, given on Tuesday, 12 July, in answer to questions by Mr Shields for APEX was that about twenty-five people from inside the Cobbold Road plant came out and joined the strike.

Shields: 'Did any incident take place?'

Bhudia: 'There was one of them, a driver and a management man, and he just tried a threat by a bottle.'

A girl named Nilam Patel, said young Bhudia, had been slapped by 'management'.

There are many charges and counter-charges about that Monday afternoon; enough has been given here to show the way the two sides felt about one another. The Scarman report, published on 25 August 1977, said 'Although there was some violence, it was short-lived – no more than an explosion of excitement following upon the Chapter Road walk-out.' The really important events, the ones that began to bring the British trade union movement and the British class struggle into this picayune revolt, took place on the following morning. Sunil Desai telephoned the Secretary of Brent Trades Council, Mr

Jack Dromey, and with that one call connected the strikers to a network of local trade union activists, tenants associations, a centre for legal advice, and all the assistance that young, passionately motivated people mostly on the left of British politics could give. The full significance of this is discussed in Chapter 5. For the moment, we need note only that Mr Dromey arrived on the Chapter Road picket line at about eleven o'clock on the morning of the second day of its existence, that he found the workers there, in his words to the Inquiry on 18 July 1977, 'like a bunch of lost chickens outside of a coop'. The lost chickens from Chapter Road and Cobbold Road were guided to the Trades Council hall nearby, where Mr Dromey told them what a union was, who APEX were, and how to elect a representative delegation to meet Len Gristey from APEX. Then he tactfully withdrew while Mr Gristey officially enrolled the new members. The goal of joining a union had been achieved, but right from the start Mr Gristey warned that he might not be able to get the Grunwick workers reinstated. APEX would, however, do its best.

Such were the humble, almost comical beginnings of the Grunwick affair. Five days after Devshi Bhudia, who had another job waiting, his young friends and Mrs Desai and her student son had walked out they found themselves with some sixty-five of their fellow-workers, thirty of them students, on their side. They could have a fair amount of confidence that as the days went by more permanent workers would join them, and gradually more did. By 31 August, the number of strikers was 137 (forty-six students), out of a total workforce of about 490. By day five the small band of strikers had managed to connect itself to Britain's powerful Labour movement. From that moment on, the Brent Trades Council, APEX, the TUC, and indeed the Labour Government felt honour-bound to use all the considerable powers at their disposal in an effort to win recognition for APEX at Grunwick and reinstatement for the workers who had walked out and who were sent notices of dismissal on 2 September.

For the strikers the struggle was not easy; at first the strike pay was as low as £8 a week and although this later rose to

£30 plus £4 from sympathizers (for some better than when they had been working), picket duty during the winter that followed, in rain and snow, day after day, was often uncomfortable, while the news was increasingly dispiriting. Every move of the trade union movement was parried by the company. The Government's Advisory, Conciliation and Arbitration Service was frustrated. A sympathy action by the Union of Post Office Workers, which 'blacked' mail to the company in November proved short-lived and futile. An appeal to an industrial tribunal failed for lack of jurisdiction. Spirits were kept up by speeches and local marches, but as 1977 wore on it seemed that there was nothing that would help except some dramatic action. That came in June, with mass picketing, the street disorders, and the headlines that led the Government to act. The long period of frustration thus ended in a collision between the supposedly irresistible Labour movement, the new Establishment, and the apparently immovable company and its friends, who said consistently that they would obey the law, no more and no less. The explosion badly frightened the Government and the TUC; they expended much energy clearing up the mess. The law could not help Devshi Bhudia and Mrs Desai and her friends, owing to deficiencies in the law for which the trade unions themselves must take much of the blame (as we shall see). Yet the company management saw no reason why it should set aside what it saw to be the rule of law, just to satisfy the new Establishment. With such a clash of principle, and powerful allies on both sides, the larger battle had to come. The Scarman report noted this, saying,

Nobody, who has studied the dispute, should be surprised that the strike has proved to be one of the longest in the recent history of industrial relations in Britain or that it persists and, with the passage of time, deepens. Its progress from small beginnings to a national issue can be seen, with the benefit of hindsight, to have been inevitable.

The Grunwick management, feeling honour-bound, used every defensive mechanism it could find. It fought in the courts, it declined repeated requests to sit down and talk. It

20

avoided the blacking of its products and the embargo on supplies of raw materials in a manner whose cleverness was reminiscent of the avoidance of economic sanctions against Rhodesia by the government led by Mr Ian Smith. In justification of this attitude it insisted that its factory was well-run and therefore not in need of a trade union or collective bargaining. As Lord Justice Scarman put it, on Friday, 22 July 1977, at the eighth sitting of his Court of Inquiry, the course of argument for the company had to be *cet animal est méchant: quand on l'attaque, il se défend* (this animal is wicked: when it is attacked, it defends itself).

The struggles that ensued, in the courts, in public institutions like the post office, in propaganda and counter-propaganda, in Parliament, and most melodramatically, in the great mock-battles between police and demonstrators in midsummer, 1977, all followed from those early decisions. So did the Scarman Inquiry, whose eventual report supported the demand of the strikers for a union and argued that ideally the company should reinstate them. The main events are listed, in chronological order, at the end of this book; the threads of the story are taken up in the chapters that follow. But first one must ask, what is it that led to such a walk-out and plea for help from a small number of disgruntled workers in a photo-processing company in Brent?

2 The people

The cause taken up by APEX was a just one: most of the Grunwick workers who followed Devshi Bhudia and Mrs Desai and her son out on strike in the week following that hot-tempered Friday in August 1976 were Asians from East Africa. Many were very young. It seems fair to assume that they knew little of the customs of most trade unions; if they had been British workers, who *should* know about those rules, APEX might have been wise to ask them, 'why come for help now? Why didn't you join a union first, and see if it could help with your grievances, and if it did not then talk about a strike?'

That APEX officials had mixed feelings about this issue is plain from the first memorandum sent by Mr Len Gristey, the London and Home Counties senior area organizer of the union, to his General Secretary, Mr R. A. Grantham. It read in part:

Grunwick Laboratories Limited,
Willesden

On Tuesday 24th August, I was contacted by a group of workers who are employed by the above company ... The work force is mainly Asian and at the Dollis Hill establishment receive £25 per week for a forty-hour week, whilst at Cobbold Road the wage is £28 per week for a forty-hour week ...

I met a very large group of the staff and pointed out to them that if they all joined the union we would first have to secure recognition and procedural rights before we could begin to talk about their conditions of employment, and this they all understood.

I further pointed out to them that for those few who were on strike or who had been sacked for taking part in a strike, there could be no guarantees whatsoever and that although we would endeavour to persuade the company to restore their jobs it was by no means certain that we would be able to do so; I also made very clear to them that we would not accept any claim for dispute benefit since this small number had chosen to take such action prior to them having approached the union . . .

Obviously the problem that now exists is the voluntary escalation of this strike by the workforce which means that most of those, if not all, who joined the union, are no longer working inside the company and it is pretty certain that the company are aware of this.

Recruitment is still continuing but frankly I suspect that the majority of the recruitment is coming from those members of staff who are joining the ranks of those already on strike. A further difficulty is that the militants amongst the Asian community are seeking to get hold of the matter for their own political purposes and this has to be watched very carefully indeed. I would be very grateful for your opinion concerning this matter.

The threat perceived by Mr Gristey receded. The unofficial strikers could be taken on because they had not yet received letters of dismissal from the company; technically they were still employed. Later the strike was made official, and benefit could be paid. It became a matter of principle that those who had been dismissed should be reinstated. The initial mixed feelings were dispelled. Perhaps one reason is that Mr Roy Grantham, according to his later recollection, reasoned that here was a badly organized section of society, a group of immigrant workers who experienced considerable difficulty in getting the normal basic British right of representation by a trade union. 'We could not walk away. If we all did that, the result would be the same situation as in America,' he said in an interview in July 1977.

Perhaps it would be similar, but it would not be the same. The East African Asian community is quite different from, say, the West Indian community and not even very like the community of Indians and Pakistanis. Among recent waves of immigration to Britain, the wave from East Africa stands out in a category of its own. Although it is often said that most of these immigrants come from Uganda, since so many were expelled by President Amin, the fact is that a large proportion of them are from Kenya. After all it was panic over Kenyan Asians that led to the Commonwealth Immigrants Act, 1968. This was rushed

23

through by the Labour Government's then Home Secretary, Mr Jim Callaghan. An essentially nationalistic measure, it introduced into British immigration law provisions whose effect was to discriminate between one British subject and another, in theory by establishing where they were born, but in practice on the ground of colour. The intention was to restrict the flow of Asians from Kenya and other East African countries. The result has been a relatively slow but nevertheless steady trickle of immigrants from these countries since then.

According to the PEP report *Racial Disadvantage in Britain,* by David J. Smith, some 15 per cent of Britain's Asian and West Indian population can be called 'African Asian', including both those born in African countries (two thirds of the total) and those born in India who stayed for a while in Africa. Unlike most other Asian immigrants, they tend to settle in London and the south-east of England. They are more fluent in English than any of the other Asian groups, and when they do find jobs (which is especially difficult for them as they are among the most recent immigrants) they are more likely than West Indians or other Asians to take on professional or white-collar work. They are least likely to do the unpopular shiftwork, and most likely to work in shops or to become shopkeepers, although the idea that they all have shops of their own is a myth. Some three quarters of the Asians in Britain are owner-occupiers, compared with only just over half the population as a whole. One reason, of course, is that coloured immigrants find it difficult to get rented accommodation; they club together or work very hard to buy cheap housing in run-down parts of a city. All these findings by PEP, which are based on research between 1972 and 1975, are supported by solid statistical evidence, which can be found in Mr Smith's report, published by Penguin Books in July 1977.

The general picture created by these statistics is hardly surprising to anyone who has known Asians in East Africa. Their energy and enterprise out there was perhaps more praised by visitors than by indigenous Africans, many of whom regarded the *dukawallahs* or shopkeepers as exploiters who charged monopoly prices. In neutral language, they were agents of economic

24

growth. A sketch of their achievements was given in a speech at a Gujerati reception in London in April 1977. The speaker was Mr Pran Sheth, deputy chairman of the Commission for Racial Equality and himself an immigrant from Kenya who works in England as company secretary to Abbey Life Assurance.

Mr Sheth told how when Britain had its Empire a large number of Indian labourers were brought to East Africa to build the railways. Contrary to popular belief in this country, he went on, few of them stayed. 'But the greater commercial opportunities and the diversity of skilled, clerical and administrative openings in the wake of colonization led, with active Government support, to an influx of Indians, principally from the west coast of India.' Within a remarkably short time the Indian settlers had created an effective network of commerce and trade, penetrating and linking the most remote parts of the country. When visiting East Africa as a young man, Winston Churchill had noted this achievement with admiration.

'Official policy aimed, as in Kenya, at creating the most advantageous situation for European colonization,' Mr Sheth continued.

'It was believed such colonization would be best achieved by assigning to the African the position of constituting a supply of cheap and plentiful labour for a commercial agriculture. The Indian was to manage retail trade, supply skilled labour, and occupy the lower clerical and administrative rungs in the railways and civil service. He was expressly excluded from the ownership of agricultural land. He was subject to a colour bar on the lines still extant in Rhodesia. Generous use was made of public revenue to set up a lavish system of education and medical services for the European settlers. Little was done for the Asians and the Africans. That seemed to them all the greater an injustice, since public revenue was raised largely through indirect taxes until the Second World War and therefore bore disproportionately on the Asians and Africans.

'Despite these severe handicaps, the Asians succeeded in setting up an impressive system of modern institutions to look after the material, moral, and spiritual welfare of members of their communities already by the twenties. They were created entirely on the initiative of the various Indian communities, being financed from their own resources. The response to the inadequate and often nonexistent government provision for their needs was, thus, to establish at considerable financial sacrifice a whole array of schools, hospitals, libraries, sports clubs, and religious cultural institutions ...

'TV news reports from Nairobi still often use the imposing domes and minarets of the Jamia Mosque proudly standing in the city centre as symbolical of it; but there are many other landmarks of Indian settlement there, from such well-endowed and modern institutions as the Aga Khan, the Social Services League hospitals, as well as schools, stadia, libraries and cultural centres. The wealth of facilities represented by these institutions is a resource on which all those who live in East Africa can draw today. But that is not merely a post-independence development. They were progressively made available to Africans even in the days when a rigid colour-bar denied European schools, hospitals and libraries to the other two races. It was Indian initiative which founded the first university institution in Kenya in the form of a college in memory of Gandhi; it became the basis for the University College of East Africa at Nairobi. In Uganda, the generosity of local Indian philanthropists and industrialists founded the first technical college and Kampala's most impressive town hall where during and immediately after the British colonial rule its parliament regularly assembled ...

'It is not easy to turn the petty trader into a heroic figure. But as historians today draw up their cold balance-sheets of the colonial chapter in the history of Kenya, the settler in the White Highlands, the dashing figure seen as the backbone of economic development, turns alas into a fantastically privileged landlord, whose contribution to the economy never succeeded in making up through export earnings the cost to the rest of the economy of supporting and subsidizing him ...

'By contrast, the Indian *dukawallah*, the butt of countless sneers, emerges as the only source of competitive enterprise in an overprotected and monopolistic economy. Working on a tiny margin of profit, marooned in remote rural areas without the most basic social services, labouring for almost impossibly long hours at the cost of personal leisure, unprotected by any security apparatus of the government, his role during the colonial period has been largely forgotten ...'

There is a heavy irony in the translation of these independent-minded and industrious people from positions of authority over African employees in Kenya, Uganda and elsewhere to jobs in England in which the trade union movement has found them to

26

be exploited by others. The important point for students of the Grunwick affair, however, is that an East African Asian workforce is likely to have retained the qualities of entrepreneurship and self-help that so marked the community's leading spirit in East Africa. People of this kind are not easily pushed around for long.

A visit to Grunwick during the height of the dispute confirmed this view. The mainly East African Asian staff of the mail-order department was interviewed – every one individually – and it was found that the group as a whole could best be described as middle-class, with a strongly motivated desire to work, and save. Most of the people who answered questions about their family circumstances turned out to be living in owner-occupied homes, with every able adult in the family working and contributing towards the mortgage. A few had managed to buy a house outright: one or two were married to successful businessmen. The husband might own two or three small supermarkets, or an estate agency, although such family wealth was rare. Only one of those questioned was living solely on the income from Grunwick, and it was clear that this was indeed a wretched case.

This broad picture of the Asians from East Africa who stayed at work applied equally to their brethren on strike: they were, after all, part of a single community. Of fifty-nine who later applied to an Industrial Tribunal for reinstatement, twenty-six were named Patel. Of the original 137 who walked out, forty-six were students – these proportions alone suggest a middle-class ambience. Young Sunil Desai subsequently went off to his studies in California. Some of the married women on strike were put under strong pressure by their husbands to return to work, and it proved necessary for the strike committee, assisted by the Brent Trades Council, to call special meetings at which the unhappy husbands were told the reasons for the strike, in an effort to win their acquiescence. In some cases, one was told, families were split: the mother might be at work, the son, a student, would be on strike.

The area of north London in which most of these Asians from Africa live is often described as run-down, a typical decaying piece of city centre. To the visitor, it seems more complicated than that. The official statistics put Brent as a city area with one of the highest concentrations of black immigrants of any borough in the country. The Scarman report speculated that about a fifth of the people of the borough might now be of 'new Commonwealth' (i.e. non-white) origin. This information is, however, not in itself useful. Among that concentration of immigrants the East African Asians are already giving every appearance of becoming an élite; it will be surprising if many of them do not move upwards from their present lower-middle class status within a very few years. If one is directed to the houses in which they live the picture is of tidiness, and pride, and an effort to bring what may have been a dilapidated property into better repair. There *are* run-down streets, but there are also good ones, new estates as well as decaying older property.

It is from this community that Grunwick began to recruit increasing numbers of workers after 1973 or 1974; the evidence as to when the process began is unclear and in the Court of Inquiry the Company denied that replacing white with non-white workers was a deliberate policy. Whatever the motives, if one bears in mind the characteristics of these people and then reads the history of Grunwick itself the surprise is that the explosion did not come sooner.

3 The company

The best place to start that history is with Mr George Ward, major shareholder and managing director of Grunwick. To listen to him tell his own story, taking some three hours off to do so at the height of the dispute (on the morning of Friday, 15 July 1977), was perhaps not a way to hear this remarkable entrepreneur at his most relaxed, but it was certainly an opportunity to witness his theatrical abilities. (He is a fair mimic, with a variety of accents from cockney to rough Irish and a pretty good Harold Wilson.) One could sense his feeling of pride in his own achievements and his outrage at the idea that others should come to interfere in the work of his company.

Born the youngest child in an Anglo-Indian family in New Delhi in 1933, Mr Ward first came to England at the age of five, but was returned to India when it was seen that war was on the way. His grandfather had been a plantation owner, but his father, at first a rich man, lost the money after investing it in Indian iron and steel, Mr Ward said. 'He lost the lot and that killed him. For that reason money is not my God. It happened to an uncle too; he was the most unhappy man I've known.' The idea of getting up at night crying 'I've lost every bean' horrified him. When his father died in 1941, his mother went out to work as a shorthand typist. He was sent to St Xavier's College, Calcutta, a Jesuit school, and then a boys' boarding school run by the Irish Christian Brothers. He hated school, and when the family returned to England in 1948 he became a postboy at a wholesale clothing company.

The restlessness of the young Ward is not hard to understand; Anglo-Indian families were either very grand or very down, back home, and there was always the difficulty of not being quite accepted by either the English or the Indian communities.

After two years as a postboy he felt he was 'getting nowhere fast'. He took a course at the Regent Street Polytechnic and then spent a year reading economics at Great Titchfield Street, apparently mastering the standard textbooks with some ease. During this time, Mr Ward said, he was living with his widowed mother in a council house in Chalk Farm.

He observed that economists seemed to find employment only with the United Nations or the Government, so in 1952 he decided to take articles for accountancy. He qualified as a chartered accountant in November 1959. 'I thought I was a genius, like all people who have recently qualified,' he recalls – many men in their mid-twenties do. He worked for a year with Messrs Farrow, Bersey, Gain Vincent and Company, but an advertisement offering a job for an accountant in Brazil caught his young imagination, and off he sailed. Arriving in Rio de Janeiro he thought 'I've made the right decision', although he knew no one and spoke no Portuguese. It was possible, while working there, for a dollar bonus to be paid to an account in New York; the net result was that he came back to England three years later with 'a nest egg'.

According to Mr Ward there was no certainty about what he would do next. One plan was to return to Brazil; another was to go into the Catholic Church. In the end he did neither, but became a partner at Burke, Covington and Nash, accountants, in 1964. The way he recalls it, he met Mr John Hickey and Mr Tony Grundy at a priory in Haverstock Hill in that same year. One day he was on a walking pilgrimage in Willesden, 'rosaries clicking', when the idea of setting up a photographic company was born. He would do the accounts, Mr Grundy the sales and Mr Hickey would take care of the production. They combined their names, the 'Grun' from the one linking to his own 'W' and the other's 'ick' to make 'Grunwick'. When Mr Ward speaks the name of the company he is very particular that the 'W' be sounded. He still goes to Mass every Sunday; Mr Roy Grantham of APEX, his principal opponent is a regular church-goer.

Such a person does not take easily to views contrary to his own, or to challenges to his power. It does not matter much whether the older Mr George Ward, by then master of Grunwick, was a *nice* man or a paternalist; the important point was that his ego seemed to the visitor to be at stake in the dispute, so that however often one asked – 'What of the rights of the employees if they happen to want to act collectively' – one simply was not heard.

Grunwick started in a mews garage in St John's Wood. It meant hard work for the three men, but it was a success. He soon gave up his accountancy partnership to work full-time for the new company. A woman who was taken on as a skilled photographic assistant in those early days remembers it as a firm in which the work was hard and the hours long, but the money not too bad. As the place grew, she recalls, someone made a joke about everyone wanting a trade union one day, to which Mr Ward is said to have replied: 'You'll get a kick up the arse.' The story may be apocryphal, but it is typical of many told by those who walked out in August 1976, some seven or eight years later. The same woman recalls that the expansion within the mews was rapid, so that adjoining garages were soon needed.

In retrospect it can be seen that the three entrepreneurs had discovered a bonanza. People seem to take photographs in good times and bad; the industry has turned out to be more recession-proof than most. By 1976 consumer spending on photo-processing in Britain had reached £120 million, a fifth more than in the previous year in cash terms, representing an 8 per cent increase in the number of prints sold. The expectation, according to market research in mid-1977, was that there would be further growth by at least as much again in that year.

Grunwick was founded at a time when the work of printing and developing still films was leaving the corner chemists' shop and moving over to the large-scale specialist companies. One of the reasons for this was the growth in the use of colour film. Small shops cannot afford the elaborate monitoring machinery which is necessary to process thousands of prints an hour, while yet providing something near to individual treatment for each one. A number of companies did well out of this technological change. One was Gratispool, in which the work built up by a husband-and-wife team played a significant part in the expansion of a section of this major European company. Another is

Tudor Processing, founded about the same time as Grunwick by two brothers, Michael and Peter de Semleyn; in September 1976 it was reported to have 600 employees, £1·25 million in processing equipment, and a fleet of over fifty vans.

To George Ward, entering this industry was 'like holding a tiger by the tail'. They started in black-and-white processing, but when the high-cost colour film market became dominant they merged with the family firm of Cooper and Pearson, who were working in colour. In the financial year ended 31 March 1975 the turnover of what was by now called GP Combined Commercial Holdings Ltd was £2·9 million. The following year it was £4·2 million, an increase of 43 per cent. Pre-tax profits grew by 19·6 per cent and trading profit by 17·8 per cent. So during the year profitability fell by nearly a fifth, if you calculate on the basis of a simple return on turnover. Yet Grunwick was still a pretty profitable business, with trading profit as a proportion of net worth 31·5 per cent in the year to March 1976 (33·3 per cent the previous year). Thus the return on capital employed was high.

The accounts show evidence of tight control, with net borrowings constant and not particularly large in relation to the size of business. No dividends were declared, which is typical of a growing private company. The growth was very fast because so much of the profit was ploughed back into the business. To any visitor the computer room, the processing equipment, the staff canteen, and the clean and bright interiors are physical evidence of this financial prudence.

The treatment of the workers

What, then, went wrong? The list of complaints about conditions at Grunwick before the strike in August 1976 was examined, item by item, in the Court of Inquiry. Let us take the main ones:

Wages, holidays and overtime

Mr Grantham alleged on the second day of the hearings that the company paid 'poverty-line wages and forced workers to work in frugal conditions'. Evidence to this effect came from APEX and the Brent Trades Council, but the difficulty is that direct comparisons between one company and another are always awkward. Working conditions, overtime, subsidized meals, and scores of other factors come into it. 'I am advised we never will find exact comparables,' sighed Lord Justice Scarman on the ninth day.

There were two wage rises after the strike, one of 15 per cent in November 1976 and one of 10 per cent in April 1977. The general consensus seemed to be that *after* those increases Grunwick was paying rather more than the rates available in similar firms. But had it been lower than the others in August 1976? Mr Grantham insisted that, 'the fact of the matter is that Grunwick were somewhat below average at that time and that they were at the bottom, or at least towards the bottom, of a low paying industry and that was one of the grievances of our members, to be judged against both the profitability and prosperity of the company as a whole'. The Scarman report accepted his premise and almost his words. 'Prior to the strike, pay was at the lower end of the rates of pay found in the by no means highly paid industry of photo-finishing,' it said.

The reader can assess the force of this from the most directly comparable of the many figures produced at the Inquiry.

According to Grunwick's own evidence, of 193 weekly paid workers, some twenty-two were paid £28 for a forty-hour week and a further thirty-two were paid £30 – all, of course, plus overtime at $1\frac{1}{4}$ times the hourly rate for the first six hours and $1\frac{1}{2}$ times the hourly rate after that. (There was double time on Sundays and public holidays.) These figures, on a sheet dated 17 August 1976, show higher rates for smaller groups of workers – fifteen of them were on £35 a week and eleven were on £45 a week, with one on £60 at the top of the scale. The average pay on this sheet was £35.60. A further ninety-seven workers were on a thirty-five-hour basic week; the twenty-one earning the least were getting £25 basic, and the average was £31.60.

A list of comparisons with pay at another London photo-processing laboratory, unnamed at the Inquiry, showed the Grunwick rates in 1976 to be roughly comparable or, at the higher end of the scales, better. For example, for splicing the range at the 'other laboratory' was £29 to £36; for Grunwick £30 to £47. Similar comparisons were made with an out-of-London photo-processing laboratory; in court Mr Grantham asked that £4 be added to these notional figures, to account for London weighting. This and other factors he mentioned complicated the issue; the most the outsider can say is that you could make Grunwick's pay look adverse by between £4 and £7 a week in 1976 on one formula, better than the other companies' by between £1 and £3 on another, and re-calculating on the formula that shows Grunwick in the best possible light, better by between £7 and £15.

These comparisons with other laboratories show Grunwick as paying relatively well in 1977, after two increases. The strikers say that the increases would not have been made if there had been no walk-out and no union. The Scarman report supported this view. But Grunwick replied with the following history of wage rate increases in the firm:

April 1973	4–23%
October 1973	4–23%
April 1974	8–15%
June 1974	16%
April 1975	11–18%
April 1976	5–13%
November 1976	15%
April 1977	10%

Increases were always of two kinds: 'all-round' and 'on merit', the latter dependent upon the opinion formed of individual workers by the managers.

The national average earnings, including overtime, for men in manual work in October 1976 was £66·97; for women £40.61. With overtime some of the women's earnings at Grunwick may not have fallen far short of the average at the summer peak. Social security depends on family circumstances; it rose to £12.70 in supplementary benefit for a single householder in November 1976. In judging the adequacy of Grunwick's rates it must be remembered that jobs were hard to come by in the area. And although a net wage of, say, £25 or £30 in August 1976 was not enough to support a family, and was hardly luxurious for an individual supporting himself or herself, for a young person living at home, or a student, or a woman helping with the mortgage it might have seemed like a useful contribution to family income.

There it is. Wages at Grunwick were certainly not generous before August 1976, and it is likely that the effect of a high turnover of staff (see below) was that a large proportion of people would be beginners and therefore on the lower or minimum rates. The counsel for APEX, Mr Stuart Shields, QC, said that before the walk-out wages 'were a source of grievance' even though not the immediate cause of what happened. This is something less than asserting that they were at starvation level; perhaps the most accurate assessment is that the company played the labour market as well as it could, to its own best advantage. And the Scarman report acknowledged that rates of pay and other financial benefits 'were not the main grievance'.

As for holidays, Mr Grantham put it to the Inquiry that, in effect, most production workers at Grunwick were entitled to only two weeks a year, since to be allowed three weeks one would have had to work there for three years and not many stayed that long. Department of Employment figures indicated that the two-week annual holiday was dead in Britain, that statistically it had disappeared. 'It may have disappeared but its head still waves pretty strongly as far as this particular company is concerned,' he said. He clearly felt very strongly about what he saw as the company's policy on holidays. For others this was not quite such a clear-cut issue as it seemed. Grunwick said that holidays accumulated at the rate of ten days per year in the first two years, and at the rate of fifteen days in the next three. The other central accusation about holidays was that they were not permitted during the summer. The company could point out that this was the peak of the season; farmers do not take holidays at harvest-time. Lord Justice Scarman observed that some people had in fact taken their holiday during the summer months, according to the tabulations of a special Gallup Poll taken at Grunwick.

Under cross-examination, Devshi Bhudia agreed that he had in fact taken a holiday between 8 and 15 August 1976, but complained that he had tried to take it at an earlier date, 'so I was disappointed'. Lord Justice Scarman commented, on the fourth day of the Inquiry, 'This happens to all of us, you know.' Was he an exception, or did others too get holidays during the summer season? Devshi Bhudia: 'only a few people who got something to prove it to the manager that you are working. I was one of the good workers, that is why they gave me the holiday, but still not at the right time.'

To be fair to Grunwick the Incomes Data Service study (no. 134, November 1976) quoted by APEX to show that the two-week holiday was a thing of the past also indicated that it is widespread practice to restrict the times when leave may be taken, at least for manual workers in private companies. The service found that there was more flexibility for most office staff, whose holidays were usually based on a roster, or some idea of 'departmental convenience'. According to this report by IDS, even for white-collar workers

The discretion is not absolute, however, and usually companies require staff workers to take their leave at certain times of the year, e.g. the United Drapery Stores Tailoring Group asks its managers to take two weeks between May and August, one week between September and December and one week between January and April.

The Scarman report had little to say on holidays.

When it came to overtime, the complaint was that it was compulsory. Grunwick agreed, but said that it was a condition of the terms of employment, since in the photo-processing business you need all the help available when the sacks of mail start piling up in the summer months. People usually wanted overtime because they could earn more that way, and, anyhow, when things were slack, in the winter, they were allowed off a few hours earlier; the union side said this time off did not amount to much. Some workers said they had to stay till ten o'clock on overtime; Grunwick said that it was compulsory until 8 p.m. but voluntary after that. The outsider who has heard all this evidence can only conclude that on most occasions the essentially hard-working East African Asians were glad of the extra money, but that there must have been evenings when they wanted to go home or to some appointment and it did not suit the management. 'Overtime . . . could easily become exceedingly burdensome, if not administered with understanding of the problems of the individual workers, many of whom were ladies with families to look after,' said the Scarman report. 'The seeds of discontent were present.' This created a grievance; the question is whether the machinery to deal with it was adequate.

Sackings

There is no doubt that there was a high rate of turnover of staff at Grunwick, at least in the mail-order department. Figures produced at the Inquiry showed that in a department with 102 employees some thirty-two people left between 1 April and 20 August 1976. Of those, twenty-one departed of their own accord, for various reasons, and eleven were sacked. Most of the departures were bunched in the six weeks leading up to the walk-out in August; in that period twenty-seven people left the department, of whom nine had been sacked.

Asked about these figures during a visit to the factory, Mr Alden leafed through his personnel records. There was a reason for every departure. 'She was an Irish girl who didn't fit in,' he said: 'she was pregnant; he went to India; he went to America; she was pregnant' . . . and so on, he said of those who resigned. Asked about the sackings, Mr Alden gave even more detailed explanations. Of the eleven dismissed, three were students. None had been with the company for longer than a year, and eight had been there for less than ten weeks. So and so had been fired for being absent without leave for two days; this person had been with the company only three days; those two had stayed away with the excuse that they could not get a bus to work (there had been a bus strike); this one had been sleeping all day; that one had handled work in a slapdash manner; this one was constantly late back from break-time visits to a betting shop; this one was very careless and dismissed after three weeks; another, 'very stroppy' although good at the job, had needed time off for a personal reason but would not take the company's offer of an extended lunch hour; so-and-so had been throwing papers at other workers; the remaining one suddenly mentioned after only six weeks that a holiday would now be taken and was told there were 'people queueing up' for a job and that the holiday should have been mentioned from the start.

There is no reason to doubt such explanations. The fact remains that no department in which a third of the staff leaves within a period of five months can be said to have settled labour relations. The writer recalls working as a dish-clearer at one of the old Lyons Corner Houses, and it is true that some people entered that particular trade for short periods when the need was pressing – but even then the company asked recruits, 'Do you intend to make a career in catering?' and there was a serious personnel policy. The atmosphere suggested by the high turnover of staff in the mail-order department at Grunwick is one in which the development of a settled, long-serving labour force was apparently not a high priority.

Immigrants

The accusation, put by Mr Shields for APEX in his closing speech to the Court of Inquiry was: 'Where you have a work-force which you find is very largely immigrant it puts you on notice, if nothing more than that, that there may be conditions here in this industry or in this factory which English or native-born workers would find unpalatable.' It is certainly true that a high proportion of the Grunwick staff was immigrant. Figures supplied by Mr John Gorst, MP, an adviser to Grunwick, show that of 206 weekly paid staff employed in the tenth week of 1977, 141 were coloured. Of these forty-one were West Indian, and seventy-eight, a third of the total, Asians mainly from East Africa. Of course if you add in the large contingent of East African Asians among the strikers it can be seen that they would have constituted the greater part of the workforce on what might be called the Grunwick shop floor.

Mr Ward said, when interviewed, that the only accusation made against him that really hurt was that Grunwick was 'racialist'. He himself, as an Anglo-Indian, had known difficulties in getting accepted in his early youth and he could not be racialist. (It is worth noting, in passing, that in spite of Mr Ward's own background, the management of Grunwick appeared to be essentially English, as did all the directors except Mr Ward.) The company could say that it was natural that it employed mainly immigrants since Brent is an area of high concentration of people from abroad; this can be only part of the explanation, however, because the proportion of immigrants in Grunwick was quite plainly very much higher than the proportion of immigrants in Brent.

The advocate who made the closing speech for Grunwick at the inquiry, Mr Stuart McKinnon, put the Grunwick response this way. The first cause of the dispute, he argued, was said to be the existence of a vulnerable labour force. 'I can deal with that in a sentence. Broadly, that may be true, but it adds nothing to the argument unless the other matters raised as causes of the dispute are of substance in themselves. Simply saying "here we have a vulnerable labour force" really does not help your Lordship.'

Management attitude

It is this charge against Grunwick that really brings all the others together. Wages may not have been generous in 1976, but that was said by APEX's own counsel not to have been an immediate cause of the dispute. The arguments over holidays and overtime did not in themselves result in a proven case that the company's behaviour was particularly oppressive of the largely immigrant labour force it had taken on. The fundamental question is whether when everyday grievances about these matters cropped up there was a way in which the workers could ask for redress. Not even the most ardent proponent of individualism can seriously hold that a recently arrived immigrant doing essentially unskilled and repetitive manual work in an area of high unemployment can argue on equal terms with a management of a prospering private company. Even if equal terms are not called for, there ought at least to be some element of fairness in resolving petty grievances. This is doubly so if a management's own attitude is disciplinarian.

Leaving aside for the moment the question of whether Grunwick's management was *excessively* disciplinarian there is no doubt that at least in the mail-order department there was an absence of any useful means of having grievances looked into. Mr McKinnon for Grunwick, to the Court of Inquiry on the tenth day: 'My Lord, it certainly was a mistake, and this is accepted by Grunwick, that there was no representation on the works committee for the mail-order department ...' In a very small company, with say twenty or even fifty workers it is likely that management and workers will be on fairly close terms, at least during office or factory hours. In a company with over 400 employees a good works committee, or something of the sort, might give individuals the sense that there is somewhere to go where they can make complaints without having to stand up to managers face to face. There *was* a works committee in Grunwicks, but it did not function for the mail-order department.

Even this might not matter if there was a happy relationship between managers and managed, but was there? Mr McKinnon said that the evidence did not support the accusation that supervisors were bullying, and prone to use the threat of the sack, or to drive workers too hard in some departments. The main thread in the evidence of the strikers was that the attitude of the management, and particularly Mr Malcolm Alden, who was in charge of the mail-order department, was too hard and aggressive. On day seven of the Inquiry Mr Alden was asked what he said about these accusations. He replied:

'I reject the allegation. I think it would be fairer to say that I maintained discipline and I caused discipline to be maintained by the managers that worked for me as much as I could, but I think that one has always endeavoured to temper the maintenance of discipline with a degree of fair play consistent with being able to produce the service that we were there to produce.'

One of the strikers' claims had been that they had had to ask permission to go to the toilet.

Mr Alden: 'I was advised – I think it was during August 1975 – by the company secretary, who is a woman and who was working with me at the time, that she had seen a number of girls in the toilet at the same time talking and chatting and this had been going on over a period of days and weeks, and I found it naturally very difficult to control or attempt to control this situation . . .'

'So what happened?'

'I told the staff that I wanted them to advise their manager or supervisor whenever they left the premises for whatever reason.'

'For how long did that last, this asking of permission?'

'It was only practical for three or four days. I think it had the effect that it let people know generally we were just a bit concerned.'

The previous day Mr Alden had told the Inquiry that after the mass walk-out on Monday, 23 August 1976, he went down to the back gates and talked to Devshi Bhudia and some of the strikers, since 'it was obvious to me that I was the object of their general excitement'.

For APEX, Mr Stuart Shields, QC, asked what they had said.

Mr Alden: 'To the best of my recollection they were things like "we cannot smoke" – I arranged that there should be no smoking – that they could not take their lunch breaks with their friends which was a coincidental arrangement, depending upon which area of the mail-order department they were working in; that they could not take their holidays when they wanted to.'

'What was the hostility towards you?'

'Devshi Bhudia was jumping up and down and calling my name, "Mr Alden, look what I have done. Me, Devshi Bhudia." This kind of hostility.'

Later in his cross-examination, Mr Shields read out a letter from a former employee, a Mrs Pushpa Rawal, to Mr Alden. It was dated 12 July 1976.

'Dear Sir, I joined the Finishing Department on 3rd May,

1976 and my service has been terminated by Mr Holden as from today.'

'I take it that must be you,' said Mr Shields to Mr Alden, reading on.

' "However, I wish that he still reconsider the decision and take me back in the service as he had not taken following points in consideration.

' "1. It was the first time I did not come to work and that is also because there was difficulty of getting to work in time.

' "2. My husband tried to get in touch with me but unfortunately the person he tried to get to inform me was having another appointment and cannot come to tell me to go to work even late. I have no phone in my house.

' "3. Mr — lied when he told my husband that there is too much work and all will leave at 7.00 p.m. Actually the dept closed at 5.30. So I presume there wasn't pressure of work.

' "4. I had still the weakness of my recent sickness and was unable to take half-an-hour walk. My husband drops me to work but on Friday the time was inconvenient for him to take me to work by car. I hope you will reconsider your decision which seems to be too harshly taken under misunderstanding." Then she says "However in case even after this plea if you are still holding up your principle please let me have my due pay and P50 form to my above mentioned address . . ." and so on, Thanking you.'

Mr Shields finished reading and addressed Mr Alden:

'This is your reply: "Dear Mrs Rawal, I am in receipt of your letter dated 12th July 1976. I do not intend to enter into lengthy correspondence concerning your ability to make telephone calls, nor your alleged recent illness. The reason for your dismissal is that you failed to report for work on Friday, 9th July 1976, and the excuse you gave was considered unacceptable. We expect our staff to make all reasonable efforts to report for work even during transport strikes.'

'Was there a transport strike?'

'That is correct. There was a bus strike for one day.'

Mr Shields read on: ' "It is quite clear that you could have got to work, living as you do only 1½ miles away. Your P45 and final pay packet will be available for collection from this office . . .'

'Would it be fair to say that is a fairly characteristic attitude of yours in these sort of matters?'

'One cannot generalize; people differ. Mrs Rawal was a different person from other employees. In the circumstances I was not able to consider re-employing Mrs Rawal. I thought it better, quite frankly, to be specific about this in my letter to her than to enter into a lengthy interchange of correspondence and maybe build up false hopes.'

That was on the seventh day of the hearings. Some time before that, on the third day, after Mrs Jayaben Desai had answered a number of questions about the manager of the mail-order department, Lord Justice Scarman said, 'You have been very fair about Mr Alden and the picture that has been created in my mind . . . is of a traditional sergeant-major type which we know very well in this country, which is by no means always a bad type.'

These back-and-forth exchanges about the management at Grunwick are important if one is to make up one's mind about the behaviour of the company. Grunwick did not bargain with a trade union. The internal mechanism for meeting grievances did not function well enough, as shown by the walk-out of 137 employees. It is clear that once a company gets to a certain size, it cannot meet current standards of what is an acceptable relationship between employer and employees if it insists that only the management has the prerogative of deciding which methods are right and which are wrong.

This seemed to be the principal flaw in the position of Mr Ward as he explained it in his three-hour interview. The way it came across, there was a going concern built from 'nothing' by the hard work and successful entrepreneurship of three able men. People who create companies like that naturally feel that what has been put together is somehow their own. There is a sense of pride in achievement, of resentment at any attempt by outsiders to interfere – and, it appeared from the interview with Mr Ward, a not necessarily ignoble desire for recognition and status in society. Allied with a strong feeling that trade union

43

power has become overweening, this led to resistance to APEX and its allies.

The Scarman report put it this way:

Since the company's attitude to unions has been the subject of discussion before us, it is right that we should state our finding explicitly. It was the desire of the directors and top management of the company, while professing to accept the right of individual employees to join a trade union, not to recognize a union for collective bargaining purposes; and they have sought up to this day to maintain that policy. They successfully resisted an attempt by the Transport and General Workers' Union to secure recognition in 1973, when a few workers (some sixteen, we were told) came out on strike in support of two who had been made redundant. They have sought up to this day to maintain their non-union shop.

Some people, reading this, might say, 'Well, what's wrong with that? That is the way of the world. That is Mr Ward's right.' In a leading article on 30 June 1977, in mid-dispute, *The Times* said that for the immigrant workers the alternative to the Grunwick type of business was unemployment.

It cannot even be said that this sort of business, of which Grunwick is not an isolated example, is exploiting the workers. These businesses could not have come into existence, or expanded if they did not have a competitive edge, and the only edge they could have is low labour costs and a willing labour force not restricted by trade union attitudes. They are not necessarily good employers, but they are employers, and if they thrive their employment practices usually improve.

The trouble with this view, which is widely held in the small business community, is that if taken to its logical conclusion in an age when deference has become an anachronism, it could stir up forces that would eventually smother all small companies. The argument may sound like good economics, but it is sociologically unsound and it is bad politics. Grunwick need not have a trade union (although the Scarman report, reflecting the views of the new Establishment, thinks it should), and if its workers do not want one it certainly should not have one, but that is not the point.

44

The point is that we live in a world in which the power employers have traditionally wielded over employees is no longer accepted by most people. New enterprises give the founders an exhilarating sense of thrust into the market and power over those who work for them. The employees are expected to feel the same excitement, and to give of their best out of loyalty to the burgeoning enterprise. 'The show must go on.' This is excellent: it is how the economy is made to prosper. But what Grunwick, Mr Ward, and those who follow *The Times* view apparently fail to grasp is that there comes a point when this no longer works. One can have the company, and, after tax, the profits – but the power, the unquestioned obedience of the workforce, is no longer available. If people insist that it must be, that will be another weapon in the hands of the anti-capitalists.

How could Grunwick have avoided this impasse? APEX will say, 'by accepting the services of a trade union and the peaceful collective bargaining that would follow'. That is one way. It is not necessarily the only way. The workers might genuinely not want a union; two opinion polls taken at Grunwick suggested that most of the Grunwick employees would rather not have one. So be it. If the employees are given collective power to balance the power of the employer through a works committee it might satisfy them; equally if the management sees to it that individual grievances do not build up that might do. Grunwick tried this, as the Scarman Inquiry noted. To keep the non-union shop, it said

they have established a works committee, and taken steps to ensure good physical working conditions. Management is 'from the front', in the sense that managers are always accessible and visible. Money has been spent on maintaining the premises in excellent condition – Chapter Road, in particular, into which the company moved in April 1976, after extensive modernization. We do, however, accept Mr Ward's statement that, if the company's workforce, or a substantial proportion of it, should evince a wish to be represented by a union, the company would not resist recognition. We also accept his word that the company recognizes the right of every employee to join a union, if he chooses. Nevertheless the company, we are sure, does all it can to persuade its employees that they are better placed without a union. There is, we stress, nothing unlawful in the company's attitude towards unionization . . .

The Scarman words seem to imply that only a union will do. This is not necessarily true, if the alternatives succeed, and are wanted or accepted by the employees.

What appeared to happen at Grunwick was that a substantial section of the workforce did not feel that there was a way of having its grievances met, either through a works committee or by individual relationships between management and managed. The balance of power was unsatisfactory. These mechanisms, whose existence is acknowledged in the above quotation from the Scarman report, did not work well enough. In modern terms this was an injustice. It is not surprising that the resilient toughened East African Asians, more accustomed by tradition to giving orders than taking them, should have rebelled against it. When they did, APEX had the decency to recognize the call.

4 The union

'When I was a clerk', wrote George Bernard Shaw in a fore-word to a threepenny pamphlet entitled *Trade Unionism for Clerks*, published in 1920, 'there were two sorts of people whom it was almost impossible to organize. First, the women. Second, the clerks.' Some trade unionists still feel the same way today. Shaw's explanation was that in the nineteenth century both women and clerks were unorganizable for the same reason. 'They did not intend to stick to their jobs. Neither of them expected to remain in the position of employee. The woman intended to get married and have a house of her own and be her own mistress, no matter how poor she was.'

As for the clerk, he 'either hated business and meant to get out of it and become a great man: poet, novelist, polar explorer, field-marshal, actor, world's champion pugilist, prime minister, or anything else in the general line of Shakespeare and Napoleon . . . or else, if he was keen on business, he meant to set up for himself unless the boss took him into partnership'. This outlook, concluded Shaw, 'made all the difference in the world between the clerk and the artisan'.

It is the change in that outlook to the more familiar one of the present, in which many women expect to be employees, or to pursue careers with no interruption save for child bearing, and in which men working in offices may see quite early on that the number of places around the boardroom table is limited, that has led modern clerks, white-collar workers, to adopt the postures of artisans. The evolution of APEX is one result of that change.

The old union of clerks

The story begins in the closing decades of the nineteenth century, when newly educated young men began to flood the labour market. By 1888 an advertisement for a clerk at a pound a week might bring 500 applications, according to Mr Fred Hughes, one of the early members of the union that is now APEX. In his published reminiscences* Mr Hughes, who became President and a lifelong official of the union, describes how in 1890 a dozen men meeting in an office in the Strand formed 'The Clerks' Union'. It has changed its name several times since then, like a public company celebrating takeover bids, or hiding the disappointment of a difficult patch. To proclaim its early spread of branches outside London it became 'The National Union of Clerks', which was soon affiliated to the TUC and the Labour Party. In 1920, after absorbing a number of other unions but taking the shock of severe internal dissensions it added the words 'and Administrative Workers' to its title; twenty years later, finally agreeing to a merger with the 'Association of Women Clerks and Secretaries', it became the 'Clerical and Administrative Workers' Union'. But it was not until 1972, when it had become the modern service conglomerate that more properly describes its main activities than the word 'union', that it chose its present long title combined with an easily remembered trade name, like Unilever or Exxon. This is 'Association of Professional, Executive, Clerical and Computer Staff', or APEX.

This analogy with large and growing business organizations is not intended as a tease of the union. The changes in character that APEX has undergone since its formation do support the proposition that what started as an earnest attempt to organize and help downtrodden clerks, carried out by men who were for the most part sincere Labour Party socialists, has developed into an institution that must fight to prosper in competition with other institutions doing the same job, like the Association of Scientific, Technical and Managerial Staff (ASTMS), managed

* By Hand and Brain: The Story of the Clerical and Administrative Workers' Union, London, 1953.

by Mr Clive Jenkins. The sincere support for the Labour Party may still be there (the socialism is perhaps less certain), but the world in which APEX lives would be uncongenial to many of its founders.

A reminder of some of the better known of these makes the point. The young Clement R. Attlee joined in 1912; he was still a member when he became Labour Prime Minister in 1945. Other early members who achieved success in Labour politics were Herbert Morrison and Arthur Greenwood. There were some oddities. In January 1910 a certain Max Harrison Litvinov was enrolled in the St Pancras branch; in 1917 he returned to his homeland to become Foreign Minister of the new Soviet republic – until he was replaced by Molotov.

The young union managed some curious successes. In 1913, Mr Hughes tells us, it got 'writers' cramp' scheduled as an industrial disease for the purpose of claims for workmen's compensation. The following year it called its first strike, which lasted for six months but fizzled out when war was declared in August.

Between the wars it probably did help to improve the general lot of clerks. But it was often embroiled in passionate political debates, about whether it should become an industrial union, or about the affiliation of Communists, who were welcome but apparently not wholly trusted; or about its latest resolution for forwarding to the Labour Party conference. In 1930, supported by Stafford Cripps, it tabled a motion in favour of the nationalization of banking, but the Party settled for the nationalization of the Bank of England.

The union of clerks was then also arguing, as APEX still sometimes does, with other unions. Around 1920 it lost many members of the Printing Trades Guild of London, which then included most of the office staffs of the Fleet Street newspapers. They went to NATSOPA, the National Association of Operative Printers and Assistants, which opened a clerical section to accommodate its victory. It argued with the National Union of Mineworkers and the Transport and General Workers' Union over rights to enrol the clerical workers when coal was nationalized; even back in 1936 writs had to be issued against ASLEF, the engine drivers' union, for the recovery of unpaid salaries of ASLEF clerks who had been off sick. But these inter-union squabbles, which are common to the histories of most trade unions, did not dim its sense of solidarity, its determination to fight for better working conditions for clerks, or the socialist convictions of many of its officials.

White-collar unions

Today the union seems less volatile than its earlier image of a combination of slightly wild political theorists might suggest. Its headquarters are in Wimbledon, in south London, a suburb in which many clerks still hope to have a house and garden. The building is flat and modern. To the visitor its sleek equipment, its working methods, and its general atmosphere suggest something quite different from the slightly bedraggled union of downtrodden clerks depicted by Mr Hughes. This is, rather, a successful corporation with nearly £1 million invested in stocks and shares and total assets of some £2·4 million, according to its balance sheet of 31 December 1976. Its net surplus of income over expenditure was £433,000 in 1975 and £480,000 in 1976. Its officials are courteous and friendly; when information was requested for this book they went out of their way to be helpful.

None of this is particularly surprising if one reflects for a moment on the business that APEX is there to do. All trade unionists are well aware that if their movement is to grow it must recruit increasing numbers of white-collar members, those very clerks and women who seemed such a lost cause to Shaw. In 1966 G. S. Bain, Director of the Industrial Relations Research Unit at the University of Warwick, estimated that white-collar workers would outnumber manual workers by the early 1980s, a forecast since supported by Department of Employment studies. This is, of course, a natural corollary of the change in most developed countries away from a heavy dependence on industrial production and towards service economies, in which central and local administrations, sales, banking, insurance, and the buying and selling of information provide more jobs than farms and factories. The artisans are being outnumbered by the clerks.

For the trade union movement this has for many years meant a danger that their influence would wane. The argument put forward by Bain and others is that traditionally the manual workers join unions in large numbers, while white-collar workers have for many years been less likely to do so. As early as 1966 Bain pointed out that if the overall level of trade union membership was to be maintained, there had to be a strong recruitment drive, especially among white-collar workers.

The trade unions have known this very well, and for some years the growth in membership of white-collar unions has been explosive. According to calculations by Bain and Robert Price, lecturer in Industrial Relations at the University of Warwick,* the number of trade unionists in traditional manual occupations has hardly grown at all since the end of the Second World War. There were just on 7·4 million of them in 1948 and just under 7·5 million in 1974. During the last four years of that period their numbers actually fell slightly. Meanwhile the number of trade union members provided by the white-collar labour force has more than doubled. There were fewer than 2 million of them in 1948, but by 1974 there were 4¼ million.

The Price and Bain figures are even more instructive when they refer to 'density' – the proportion of the total available workforce that is in trade unions. Among manual workers this rose from 50·7 per cent in 1948 to nearly 58 per cent in 1974, largely because more women manual workers joined unions. The increase in 'density' – degree of unionization – among the white-collar workers was greater: it rose from 30·2 per cent in 1948 to 39·4 per cent in 1974. Again, the larger the company the more likely it is to be unionized; companies with fewer than 200 workers may well not be.

Most traditional trade unions have adjusted themselves to the new world of white-collar unionism. There are clerical, technical or supervisory sections in the three largest unions, the Transport and General Workers' Union, the Amalgamated Union of Engineering Workers, and the General and Municipal

* *British Journal of Industrial Relations*, November 1976, p. 339.

Workers' Union. On top of this the white-collar unions themselves have recruited heavily, perhaps doing better in years when the law especially favoured them, as under the Labour Government of 1968–70, than in years when it did not, as under the Conservatives' Industrial Relations Act of 1971–4, but in any case doing very well indeed.

The National Association of Local Government Officers (NALGO) grew from 440,000 members at the end of 1970 to 683,000 at the end of 1976. Mr Jenkins' ASTMS, which had nearly tripled its size to 220,000 by 1970, had 374,000 on its books at the end of 1975 and, according to Mr Jenkins, some 400,000 a year later. In such a climate APEX could hardly fail to thrive. In fact its growth has been steady rather than spectacular, especially when set against that of its arch rival ASTMS. The old Clerical and Administrative Workers' Union had 35,525 members in 1948 and 79,870 in 1968. At the end of 1976 APEX had 141,766. Thus the 1970–76 growth rate of APEX, at 40 per cent, was about half that of ASTMS in the same peroid.

The new APEX

When the world in which it operates is in a state of such ferment any institution will naturally concern itself about its own overall purposes. Since more than half the members of APEX are clerks in the engineering industry, there is a lobby within the union in favour of turning it into the staff section of the Amalgamated Union of Engineering Workers. Mr Roy Grantham, the General Secretary of APEX, who is technically an employee of the union's executive, but in fact a strong leader, does not support such a policy. He joined the Clerical and Administrative Workers' Union as an official in 1949, his previous job having been executive officer in the civil service. He rose steadily within the ranks, but it was a surprise to some when he was appointed General Secretary in 1970, since it did not at that time appear to be quite the moment for this particular Buggins' turn. Perhaps the reason why he was chosen is explained by what he did next. For it was Mr Grantham who set off the internal review that led to the creation of APEX. The purpose of the new structure would be to widen the spread of members both among industries and in different occupations. The conglomerate was set for growth. Since the market-place already contained other, powerful suppliers, this would not be easy, but Mr Grantham, who has the demeanour of a determined, not to say stubborn, chief clerk, did not seem to be daunted. It is a commonplace in trade union circles that Mr Grantham and Mr Clive Jenkins of ASTMS are not fond of one another, and it may be that there is an element of institutional rivalry in the behaviour of the organizations they both serve as paid chief executives, but it would be shallow to assert that this is the whole explanation of what both of them have done in the drive for growth.

Yet there have been clashes. The most serious one in the recent history of the union came after a 1970 merger with the old Union of Insurance Staff and ASTMS. This led to ASTMS recruiting members of the staff of the General Accident Corporation. The response of many of the employees was to form Staff Association General Accident, or SAGA. This one-company union never became affiliated to the TUC, but it did find itself in hot competition with ASTMS for staff. In March 1974 SAGA decided to merge with APEX, which the clerical union accepted as a perfectly logical consequence of Mr Grantham's policy of extending coverage to other industries and among all grades of white-collar workers. The trade union movement has a set of rules for dealing with this kind of dispute, and ASTMS complained to the TUC that these rules – the Bridlington Principles – had been broken by APEX.

The rest of this little tale well justifies the word saga. After a seemingly interminable and certainly tedious series of exchanges, the special disputes committee set up by Mr Len Murray, General Secretary of the TUC, found in favour of ASTMS. It appeared that Mr Jenkins had won and Mr Grantham had lost, for one of the cardinal unwritten understandings within the movement is that you bow down under such decisions, especially when, as in this case, they are endorsed by the TUC Congress. Mr Grantham, who does not easily bow down, fought on, although APEX formally agreed to expel the former

SAGA members. Then the worst sin possible, from the TUC point of view, was committed by SAGA: it went to court. Worse still, it won, gaining a decision in October 1975 that APEX could not expel the SAGA members so that they could join ASTMS. To most people in the TUC the technical point that it was SAGA (or, strictly, its former chairman) who went to court did not erase from their minds the association of APEX with such an unheard-of breach of custom and practice.

Partly for this reason APEX is not popular among its fellow members of the TUC. There are other reasons. Mr Grantham is staunchly in favour of Britain's membership of the European Economic Community. He campaigned vigorously and publicly for a 'yes' vote in the 1975 referendum on this issue, going so far as to appear on a platform with the former Conservative Prime Minister, Edward Heath. His union is regarded as 'right-wing', although it would be more accurate to say that it does not associate itself with the left-wing of the Labour movement.

There is plenty of evidence for this. The president of APEX, Mr Denis Howell, is the Labour Minister who turned out to be so good at bringing the rains down when he was made responsible for measures to alleviate the drought in 1976; he is also firmly identified with the right of the Party. So are Mrs Shirley Williams and Mr Fred Mulley, other APEX-sponsored Members of Parliament who have become Ministers. (When a member is 'sponsored' the union pays the salary of the election agent.) The Chancellor, Mr Denis Healey, is one of twenty-six members of the APEX parliamentary panel, which has the approval of the union's annual conference. Half this panel are MPs; the amount of support given to them is less than for sponsored members. A look at these thirteen, and the list of sixteen other Labour Party members of APEX in the House of Commons may show some left-wingers, but it is names like those of the non-left Mr Harold Lever that tend to stand out. There are also three Conservatives, including Mr Jim Prior, Tory spokesman on employment, although those receive no support, moral or financial, from the union.

Early in 1977 the Labour Party itself was deprived of additional financial support from the substantial political fund of

APEX. This happened when Mr Andy Bevan was appointed national youth officer of the party. APEX, complaining of 'infiltration' and 'entryism in the Party of extremist groups' stated: 'The Executive Council of the Union cannot agree to the contribution of our members who pay the political levy being used for purposes which are alien to the cause of a democratic Labour Party or to finance the activities of Trotskyist groups within the Party.'* (Thus the union would give no money, other than affiliation fees, while the Labour Party took no action against 'entryism'.)

The money in the political fund, the article went on, would only be used to support members of APEX in elections, 'since we are satisfied that all the members supported by the Union politically, support the democratic principles upon which the Labour Party was founded and upon which it must continue to progress in future'.*

This is not the only evidence of the anti-extremist character of APEX. Its own officials calculate that in internal elections what is seen as the 'right' usually wins about two thirds of the vote, and thus most of the contests. It is one of the very few unions to maintain a list of proscribed organizations; any member belonging to one of these must declare his or her membership when standing for election for union office or as a representative of APEX on outside bodies. Among the proscribed bodies are the Communist Party, an internal ginger group called APEX Action, the Socialist Workers' Party, other similar fringe left parties, and the National Front and the National Party on the right. The Westminster Trade Union and Political Staff branch of the union, whose energetic secretary, Mr Chris Wright, is certainly in sympathy with the Tribunite left of the Labour Party, was especially militant during the Grunwick dispute, so much so that at the end the branch was severely critical of the union leadership for what it regarded as back-pedalling. Yet although this was a factor in the Grunwick case, such attitudes are atypical of the union as a whole.

APEX members do support the Labour Party in large numbers, if the union's high level of individual contributions to

* *APEX*, vol. 15, no. 1.

the political levy is any guide, but by and large they seem to be a moderate lot. In the 1972 miners' strike many clerical workers for the Coal Board crossed the National Union of Mine-workers' picket line; in one famous incident in Doncaster the miners spat at the girl clerks as they walked through. In the 1974 miners' strike there was support for the NUM by APEX clerical workers, although not all of them obeyed the executive's injunction not to cross the lines. The reasons behind such divisions are of course not merely political: there is a traditional divide between office staff and pit workers in the mining industry and even the clerical section of the NUM, which has more members in the coal industry than APEX, was reportedly not able to bring out all its clerks in 1972.

But incidents of this kind do show that at the advancing frontiers of its expansion the 'moderate' APEX must inevitably run into trouble with its brethren in other unions. In 1974 Mr Hugh Scanlon, President of the AUEW, called in the police to escort fourteen of *his* staff through an APEX picket line, at a time when APEX and TGWU office staff working at Mr Scanlon's headquarters were on strike over a pay claim.

The end result of the consequent unpopularity was that Mr Roy Grantham lost his seat on the General Council of the TUC and with it went some of the prestige and influence of APEX inside the union movement. The Grunwick strikers found their way to APEX at a time when the union, embarked on a policy of growth but perhaps unsettled by the troublesome course of its affairs during the previous two years, may well have been caught off-guard.

It may never be possible to be certain of this. To say that APEX simply saw a chance to win new recruits if Grunwick could be mopped up is too simple; the time and energy needed to recruit the small numbers available at the photographic company seem disproportionate for so businesslike a service conglomerate as APEX. The decision to defend coloured immigrants at what would plainly be a high cost was clearly a moral one, for which Mr Grantham and APEX surely deserve high credit. The Grunwick employees were APEX's first members in the film-processing industry. 'In our own view,' said the Scar-

56

man report, 'there was no political motivation or "empire building" on the part of the union. The union was not looking for members: some Grunwick employees were looking for a union.' Perhaps there was a mixture of motives. If the Grunwick dispute could be won by APEX, it might open up a new field of recruitment among immigrant workers; it would anyway set a precedent for similar recognition demands at the many small companies that still remain to be unionized. Individually these companies may not mean many new members, but collectively they constitute one of the few remaining places to go. The Price and Bain analyses makes this quite clear, since they pinpoint the type of large company (in banking, perhaps, or insurance) and the size of small company that a white-collar union anxious for growth should be tackling. The new Labour laws giving the unions a specially favourable opportunity to pursue claims for recognition made August 1976 the right time to act. Such long-term calculations may not have been to the forefront when the Grunwick file fell on Mr Grantham's desk, but they are part of the everyday assumptions of a union like APEX.

Even so, it was not predictable that this non-left successor to a somewhat raffish union of clerks should stumble into such a troublesome quarrel, apparently led by the nose by a decidedly left-wing organization of a quite different nature, the Brent Trades and Labour Council.

5 The Brent connection

Trades councils are easy pickings. Anyone in the Labour movement will confirm this. Small groups of people willing to sit
through interminable committee meetings and conferences can,
with persistence, ensure that those of a certain cast of mind win
most of the elections to positions of responsibility. It is probably easier to take over a trades council than a constituency
Labour Party, and the successive coups by left- and right-wing
groups within the Labour Party at Newham in 1974–7 has
shown how easy *that* is.

The councils are easy to pick off because they are really as-
semblies of delegates from trade union branches. Those
branches are often little more than empty shells, ready for any
group to fill. There is no money and little glory in winning
election from a local branch of a trade union to the local trades
council, although this may not have been true in the days when
the branches themselves had some local autonomy. Those days
are gone: as long ago as 1968 the Donovan Commission pointed
out (paragraph 116) that many trade union branches consist of
small groups of members from a number of different factories
or offices, and commented that 'The branch is therefore divorced from the real business of the union at the place of
work . . .'

It is a relatively simple matter, therefore, for people of a
given political persuasion, left or right, to sit through a sparsely
attended meeting of a trade union branch until the time comes
to vote upon their own particular slate of delegates to the
Trades Council. For the left wing of the Labour Party it is even
easier, since in the absence of organized challenges from the
ultra-left revolutionary groups, the people who attend trade
union meetings will likely as not be in sympathy with what is

58

known in those circles as the 'broad left' (that is, not quixotically ideological), even though there may be a majority of conservative-minded individuals among the rank and file members.

It is thought in Brent that of forty-two trades councils in Greater London perhaps half a dozen have been taken over by one or other of the wild schismatics of the 'ultra-left', with most of the rest in the 'broad left' camp. Of course 'broad left' will include people associated with the left wing of the Labour Party plus modern-style Communists – the kind who insist that they have no intention of imposing totalitarian rule should they get the chance. Most people will be Marxists but not Stalinists. These distinctions may seem obscure to non-left outsiders, but to those in the business they are crucial.

The conspiracy theory

Before considering where Brent Trades Council fits into this odd corner of our political life it is important to note one common accusation about such groups: that they conspire to create industrial disputes. When one thinks about it, this is highly improbable. There *may* be cases where a single individual or group has stirred up feeling or where plotters have created conditions leading to a strike, but before believing accounts of any of them it would be necessary to examine the evidence with great care. The reason is that large numbers of people do not usually come out on strike, or stay out on strike, if they do not have a genuine grievance. When Mr S. Sedley, counsel for the Brent Trades Council, argued before the Court of Inquiry on Monday 18 July that 'no amount of exhortation or propaganda will induce thousands of workers to sacrifice a day's pay or take a day of their holiday entitlement in order to come and support a picket on the gates of a small factory which nobody had heard of a year ago' he may have been underestimating the powers of his clients to whip up such support, but his general proposition was surely sound.

In the Grunwick case there *must* have been an initial sense of grievance, since 137 workers walked out in response to the lead

59

given by Devshi Bhudia, Mrs Desai and the others. There is no evidence that that action was the result of a left-wing plot or indeed any other deep-seated conspiracy; certainly this accusation was not made at the Inquiry.

It is true, as will be seen, that the subsequent course of the dispute was partly influenced by the Brent Trades Council but it would be absurd to argue that so much trouble would have occurred if there had been no underlying sense that justice would not be done until APEX was recognized and the strikers were reinstated.

Yet even those of us who generally reject the conspiracy theory must note the remarkable cohesiveness of people 'active in the community' in Brent. The description of how they are brought together is like that old song,

> The thigh bone's connected to the
> hip bone,
> The hip bone's connected to the
> back bone . . .

Mr Jack Dromey, the bearded, twenty-eight-year-old practitioner of industrial politics in Brent, is disarmingly open about this. As a member of the Transport and General Workers' Union, Kilburn Branch (presumably a white-collar member since his paid employment is 'community liaison and development officer' at the Brent Community Law Centre), he is an elected delegate to the Brent Trades Council. In 1973 he became secretary of that council. The Brent Trades Council sends Mr Dromey as a delegate to the Greater London Association of Trades Councils, where he has risen to a seat on the executive committee. That association sends him as a delegate to the South East Regional Council of the TUC; there, too, Mr Dromey came to sit on the executive committee until in May 1977 he was elected secretary of SERTUC, a body which, in his words 'covers an area stretching from the Wash to Portsmouth and represents the four million trade unionists in the south east'.

So far there is nothing more intricate in this than, say, an interlocking series of company directorships, with about as much attention paid to the election of officials in the ever-ex-

60

tending circles of trades councils as most shareholders pay to the election of company directors, with perhaps more competition on election to SERTUC than lower down. But the Brent connections are wider than the account given so far might suggest. As a member of the executive committee of the National Council for Civil Liberties for seven years and chairman in 1975–6, Mr Dromey served an important national pressure-group. The Community Law Centre was partly his own creation; it derives its authority from local community organizations, like tenants' associations, in a manner not dissimilar from the trades council.

There is yet more. The Brent Trades Council is elected by seventy-four local trades union branches, with a collective membership of 21,000. Conscious of the usual divorce between trade union branches and the members of local unions, the council has developed what its chairman, Mr Tom Durkin, described to the Inquiry as 'close links' with local shop stewards' committees and some district and regional trades union organizations. It does not stop there. The links have been forged with 'some local authority committees, the Brent Federation of Tenants' Associations and its environmental committee, the Brent District Community Health Council . . . the Harlesden Advice Centre, the Active Old Age Pensioners' Committee, Brent Women's Centre and some other bodies'. Still the connection goes on. 'We are also represented on the District Manpower Committee, the Community Relations Council and the Brent Campaign against Racism which we played a leading part in setting up.'

Such links bring the office-holders of the Trades Council into contact with a great many people. Mr Dromey to the Court of Inquiry, July 1977: 'For example, personally, I sit on the Brent and Harrow District Manpower Committee, of which I am vice-chairman. The chairman is the personnel manager of Heinz. I also sit on the Brent Community Relations Council, the Brent careers service sub-committee of the education Committee of the London Borough of Brent and the West London Supplementary Benefits Appeals Tribunal.'

In short, the Brent Trades Council appears to have its own

immediate area pretty well sewn up. This may be atypical of trades councils in general, but it could be true of Brent. Mr Dromey: 'As secretary, I am in daily contact with the highest paid, most skilled and best organized sections of the working class in Brent.' There is nothing necessarily sinister in this. The Brent connections do give ambitious individuals a chance to make their names more widely known, and the reward of local power and standing in the community is certainly available, but it is hard to see how such a network could be created without dedicated hours of often tiresome work by people whose sincere motivation is, presumably, the advancement of the working class. Some of their work in Brent, particularly in race relations, should surely be acknowledged as valuable by those outside the left who understand the dangers of racial conflict in such a multi-racial area.

On paper, Trades Councils are simply local coordinating committees that represent the interests of individual trade unions in a particular place. For this reason it was, on paper, only natural that a day or so after his meeting with the newly-enrolled members of APEX on Tuesday, 24 August 1976, Mr Len Gristey should have asked Mr Jack Dromey and the Brent Trades Council for all possible support in handling the dispute. He certainly got it, even before he asked. It was Mr Dromey who, through Mr Eric Boon, an APEX branch official who also happens to be vice-chairman of the Brent Trades Council, had arranged for the production of APEX membership forms at the Trades Council hall that Tuesday night.

No doubt Mr Len Gristey's opinion of Grunwick was shaped from the very beginning not only by the tales told by the strikers, his new members, but at least in part by the picture put before him through the Brent connection. To the outsider it appears that this must have been an important ingredient in setting the tone for Mr Gristey's report back to APEX headquarters, and the consequent decisions taken by the APEX executive.

An idea of the sort of news he must have received in those early days can be gleaned from the statement of Mr Tom

Durkin, the Trades Council Chairman, at the Inquiry. He himself had been involved through his council in picketing and organizing support for Transport and General Workers' Union members who had been sacked by Grunwick early in 1973.

'This strike lasted, I believe, for a period of eight weeks and was beaten. A small number of Grunwick workers in Cobbold Road were then in the Transport and General Workers' Union and about thirty others wanted to join this union,' said Mr Durkin. 'The sackings and the defeat of the strike ended this attempt to unionize Grunwick.' That incident marked the company down as anti-union, at least in the minds of some trade unionists in Brent.

There are other, independent, reasons why Mr Gristey's first reports to Mr Grantham will have indicated that here was a tough employer and a difficult situation. On 26 August 1976, he went along to Grunwick to approach the company direct. He had in mind recent protest marches by Asian immigrants in Southall, and thought the mood of the crowd outside the door, a crowd which in his view included some who were not strikers, 'was certainly not too cool'.

Then, Mr Gristey told the Court of Inquiry, he was stopped outside Grunwicks by a constable, 'who frankly caused me to laugh at first when he said that he would not allow me to go and knock on the company's door because he would not answer for my safety, which is something I have never experienced before in this country, where I could not walk up to any employer's door and knock on it'. Such was the atmosphere outside.

'When the two gentlemen from the company finally came out they protested very violently to me – vehemently would be a better word – about incidents they claimed had happened over the past day or so ... I said that I would make sure that from our side matters were cooled off.' He told Mr Stacey and Mr Pearson, the company representatives, his view of the feeling in the crowd, reporting that one or two had said as he came through that there could be a further Southall march, this time in Willesden.

That emotionally charged exchange was the only meeting

ever held between the management of Grunwick and Mr Gristey, the representative of APEX, according to Mr Gristey's evidence at the Inquiry nearly eleven months later.

This formative experience apart, Mr Gristey and APEX were well plugged in to the Brent switchboard. Mr Dromey helped organize a picket system and a rota for the pickets. He took the strikers to local factories to put their case to workers whose support might be helpful later. The Trades Council organized four local marches and several public meetings including one on 12 December at which the main speaker was Mr Len Murray, General Secretary of the TUC. Help was given with the production of regular strike bulletins and press statements, and strikers who wanted legal advice were welcomed at the Community Law Centre. But there was more to the Brent connection than that.

For Mr Jack Dromey worked quickly to turn his 'bunch of lost chickens outside of a coop' into a forceful group of strikers. On 18 July 1977, he described how to the Court of Inquiry:

'For the first month of the dispute we had daily members' meetings, followed by committee meetings. This was unusual but necessary because the strikers were so inexperienced . . .' He and Mr Gristey attended many of the strike committee meetings, naturally as non-voting members. It does not take much imagination to see that the local man, who was not only at the centre of the Brent connection but who had lived in the area all his life (for parts of the time only a few hundred yards from Grunwicks), would be best able to impress the inexperienced strikers with his ability to get things done. Both APEX and the Trades Council had taken on something new to the experience of the officials immediately involved, but the Trades Council was temperamentally more likely to favour hard 'industrial action'.

The unsteady relationship developed erratically during the subsequent eleven months, with the Trades Council on occasion leading APEX from behind and APEX at times apparently unable to exert discipline over its own strike committee. The strategy adopted from the start was 'to take the issue into the trade union movement'. Mr Dromey to the inquiry: 'This was necessary because we recognized the importance of the issues involved in respect of trade union rights and the status of immigrant workers in this country, and because it was clear that the industrial muscle of the strikers was limited.' Making the trade union movement responsive to the Grunwick strike was hard work, but quite possible for any committee that started off with the advantages of the Brent connection. They sent letters to all possible sympathizers. They despatched delegations of strikers on tours of the country. Speakers, displays, and workers from Grunwick were sent to most major trade union conferences. Articles were written for journals read by people in the movement.

'Well before the mass picketing ever began, Grunwick had become a household name within the organized trade union movement.' said Mr Dromey in his statement of 18 July 1977. 'By March of this year there was a widespread feeling within the trade union movement that the remedies for the union and the strikers were totally inadequate and that an industrial approach was the only way of winning the demands of recognition and reinstatement.'

Within that movement left-wingers would doubtless have been in the forefront of arguments to the effect that tackling Grunwick by means of ordinary picketing, an approach through the Advisory, Conciliation and Arbitration Service, and traditional 'blacking' of the company's products were not good enough to get the results they wanted, or to defend the trade union movement against a new challenge to its power. The picketing in fact fell away to token size during much of the winter, and it took an APEX executive decision and an effort of will by the strike committee to step it up to a twenty-four-hour picket, manned with the assistance of sympathetic outsiders after Easter 1977.

The argument in Brent, as elsewhere, was that Grunwick was out to defeat the union movement, since it had accepted the assistance of the National Association for Freedom (see next chapter) an organization whose purpose the unions saw as the creation of a federation of small businessmen, the self-employed and professionals to form a third force that would interpose itself between the TUC and the Confederation of British Industry. Mr Dromey: 'The view within the trade union movement was and is that the NAFF is seeking to whittle away the hard-won rights of trade unionists and to become a new "employers' association" for companies like Grunwick.'

With such a force behind it, as APEX could argue and its Brent associates would no doubt rub home, Grunwick was in their view able to spin out the legal processes available through the ACAS under the Employment Protection Act (see Chapter 10). The official boycott of Grunwick's post in November 1976 was halted after a court action (see Chapter 12). The frustration and anger mounted.

The Brent view was that APEX should ask the TUC to arrange with other unions that all supplies and services to Grunwick should be cut off until it recognized the union and took back the strikers. Mr Dromey: 'Then on Monday March 7th [1977], at a meeting organized by the South East Region of the TUC, the Greater London Association of Trades Councils and the No. 8 District London, of the Confederation of Shipbuilding and Engineering Unions, Roy Grantham announced that he was going to make such an approach to the TUC. I chaired that meeting.' In the event the TUC did ask that APEX be given all assistance possible, but the powers of the Brent connection are limited to its immediate and rather special circle of contacts. This apparently does not include the water and electricity workers, for the strikers' hopes that these essential services to the factory would be cut off were not realized.

An explanation for this breach of solidarity was forthcoming in July 1977, when, following the mass picketing and the shocks this created, Mr John Lyons, General Secretary of the Electrical Power Engineers' Association, put what may well have all along been the view held by many rank and file trade unionists. In a report in his association's journal, he said:

The dispute at Grunwick has become a major national issue. A report appeared in the May issue of the *Electrical Power Engineer*, when the circular issued by the General Council of the TUC was reproduced. That circular had been considered by the National Executive Committee immediately before Conference, when it was agreed to donate £500 to APEX to assist them in their efforts to obtain recognition at Grunwick.

When the NEC agreed to that donation, they did so because they felt that it was right to respond to the TUC's appeal on behalf of a union which was faced with its members having been dismissed for having joined a union; and further, the same employer both refused to recognize the union or accept a recommendation by ACAS that the union should be recognized. The employer refused ACAS the facility to ballot his own employees on whether or not they wished APEX or any other union to represent them.

Since the NEC made that decision, there have been developments which have severely clouded the original issues and greatly disturbed many – I would judge the overwhelming majority – in the trade union movement. I refer to the mass picketing at Grunwick and the use made of this by certain elements seeking to turn it into a political confrontation and to gain personal and political publicity from it unrelated to the purposes of the action itself. The general atmosphere of intimidation to which this has given rise has done the trade union movement a great deal of harm.

So has the attempt to cut off basic supplies to Grunwick. The NEC had been asked to cut off electricity supplies to Grunwick at the same time as it considered financial support. This the NEC were not prepared to contemplate. Other unions in the industry have also been asked, and have reacted similarly. The view of the National Executive Committee is quite clear. Our members have a statutory obligation to supply electricity to the community without discrimination, and no matter what the intrinsic merits of other disputes there could never be any question of our Association calling on its members to set aside this basic obligation. Nor would our members respond. Once started down this road we would indeed be on the highway to anarchy.

The genuine issue at Grunwick remains. It was worth our support to begin with, and continues to be worth it now. It is that employees have a right to choose to belong to a union and seek recognition through legal procedures laid down by Parliament. They should not be sacked for apparently exercising that right even if they are on strike over an industrial dispute. On that issue we must continue to support APEX in its effort to establish the reality of this right by lawful means.

At APEX, and in Brent, the view was not quite so measured. The union side was faced with the apparent recalcitrance of the

67

company; the threat, as they saw it, of the movement against trade unionism represented in their minds by the NAFF; and a forced withdrawal from what had been regarded as a promising field for recruitment of trade union members among small companies and immigrant workers. How much industrial muscle was required to overcome this? In some minds the struggle became a test case. Win this one and NAFF would have suffered a grievous defeat, while other small companies would take the point and immigrant workers would come flocking in as members. Lose it, and NAFF would be triumphant, the small companies of Britain would become doubly stubborn, and immigrant workers would feel once again that the trade union movement was not for them.

Putting things in such apocryphal terms is natural to politically minded left-wingers, of the kind found in Brent; after all many of them see society through Marxist eyes. There may have been similar debates inside the APEX headquarters, or at the TUC, but the stark clarity with which these momentous issues were presented will have been highlighted by the Brent connection. That sort of thing is, after all, their business.

In the opinion of the Brent workers the Easter call by APEX for twenty-four-hour-a-day picketing 'was too generalized'. It did not succeed in spite of efforts by the several organizations and unions with whom the Trades Council had close links. According to Mr Dromey's account, Mr Grantham then came down to the Trades and Labour Hall in Brent early in May to meet the strike committee in an effort to arrange a better plan.

Since the general call for mass action had failed, it was decided that a specific call for a mass picket should be made for the week beginning Monday, 13 June 1977. The decision was subsequently ratified by the executive committee of APEX. Apparently, it was thought at the time that perhaps a few hundred people might turn up; in the event the thousands that arrived after the first day provided a form of nightly theatre on TV that must have severely damaged the trade union movement and the Labour Government in the eyes of the wider electorate whose existence may not always be fully appreciated among political–industrial activists. It was for this reason that later on in the dispute the natural rift between the militant Brent Trades Council, the strike committee and Mr Wright's branch of APEX on one side and the moderate leadership of APEX itself on the other widened. At the top, the Labour Government, the TUC, and APEX could not risk future clashes on the streets; in Brent it was the 'mass industrial action' that alone had brought them nearer to victory.

Much of the account of the Brent connection in this chapter is based on Mr Jack Dromey's statements to the Court of Inquiry. In private conversation, Mr Dromey said that he would call himself a Marxist. He had no political affiliation except to the Labour Party, but he shared the Marxist view of history and the Marxist economic analysis. He was not an 'entryist' (or, to the non-political outsider, an infiltrator). His belief was, however, that it was best to cultivate the broadest possible political base; this is consistent with private indications from other protagonists to the dispute that the Brent Trades Council discouraged the involvement in the Grunwick dispute of 'ultra-left' parties, even though those parties did turn up on the picket lines and did create a large amount of disturbance.

The view inside Grunwicks during the dispute was that Mr Dromey was building himself a political future by his actions. The description of the Brent connection in this chapter might be consistent with that view, and it may be that while people not on the left might see the Brent connection as a usurpation of power by Marxist-minded activists, many trade unionists and Labour Party supporters on the left would see it as evidence of strong organizing ability. Thus to accept the picture presented by Mr Durkin and Mr Dromey to the Court of Inquiry might simply be to retail an advertisement by the Trades Council. Perhaps it is, but the balance of probability seems to be that if you start with a moderate service conglomerate like APEX and have it asked, out of the blue, to help some bewildered young strikers at Grunwick, you do not land up with the later confrontation on the streets if there is no volatile ingredient like the Brent connection present and ready to set the explosive processes going. There was, of course, another volatile ingredient, the NAFF.

6 The National Association for Freedom – and the Conservative Party

The National Association for Freedom is a crusade, or it is nothing. It is as unhelpful to regard it as a conspiracy as it would be to assert that the idealists behind the Brent connection were merely conspirators. There is a sincere philosophy behind the organization known as the NAFF, and it is one that has a long, respectable history of Western liberal philosophy behind it, not to mention a strong connection with contemporary thinking inside the Conservative Party, at least in the wing represented by leaders such as Sir Keith Joseph and Mrs Margaret Thatcher.

Yet the most passionate adherents of this mode of thought clearly feel themselves to be so beleaguered, so much a minority in the world of politics and the press, that they stimulate suspicion of their motives by being less than wholeheartedly open and frank about themselves. This particular characteristic was to some people as true of Mr Ward as it is of the NAFF which did so much to support him. For example, in the High Court case against the Advisory, Conciliation and Arbitration Service the trade union and ACAS proved willing to disclose their own internal documents and memoranda, as did APEX before the Court of Inquiry under Lord Justice Scarman. But when, on the ninth day, Mr Stephen Sedley, for the Brent Trades Council, asked Mr Ward whether Grunwick was willing to disclose to the Court its board minutes concerning the dispute the reply was that the company was not prepared to do anything other than the law required.

In the case of the company there are some pieces of information that it would naturally want to keep confidential in order to survive; for example, its methods of obtaining materials in spite of the attempted 'blacking' of supplies by trade unions. It is probably also true that some private information about the unions and their allies was not disclosed in court, or elsewhere. Yet the impression remains. In preparing material for this book every organization that was approached on the trade union side responded with what seemed to be complete openness and a willingness to provide a full answer to whatever was asked. With the reservations about what might be called 'defence-restricted' material Mr Ward and Grunwick, advised by Mr John Gorst, MP, seemed to be nearly as willing to meet all this reporter's questions, even if at the Court of Inquiry they stood by the letter of the law.

The NAFF was the least open. Two of its three leading figures were approached. Mr Robert Moss, a director, tried to be helpful, but that is the end of the story. There seemed to be a feeling that any inquirer who could not be relied upon to support the NAFF view could not be relied upon at all. This is not an unusual experience in any reporter's life, but it is worth noting in the present instance as evidence of the way the organization behaves within what must appear to its founders to be a hostile environment. That said, we must look at what the NAFF does in fact stand for.

Throughout 1975, there had been plans afoot to form some kind of organization based on the ideals of the National Association for Freedom. The murder of Ross McWhirter, who with his twin brother Norris was well-known as co-author of *The Guinness Book of Records*, settled all the arguments about its nature. Five days after that tragic event, on 2 December 1975, the association was formally launched.

According to Mr Moss a coherent exposition of the thinking behind the NAFF can be found in his book, *The Collapse of Democracy*, first published by Maurice Temple Smith in 1975 and subsequently brought up to date in a 1977 edition published by Sphere Books Ltd. It is not possible to summarize such a long and complete work in a few paragraphs, but some of the points relevant to the NAFF role in the Grunwick dispute are plain.

Mr Moss sets out four propositions, outlined in his introduction. The first is that advocates of undemocratic forms of society can destroy democracy through its own institutions. Presumably this means that if, say, the Communist Party wins an election in Italy and behaves as Communist Parties in Eastern Europe have behaved when in power, Italian democracy would be destroyed. Second, Mr Moss argues, there are certain preconditions for the survival of democracy: in his view these include 'economic democracy', i.e. the maintenance of a 'strong private sector', and a press that is not 'gagged'. Democracy is also threatened, he says, 'if a monopoly social pressure group is able to assert its own interests at the expense of the community at large'.

Mr Moss's third proposition is that 'the threat from totalitarian movements and ideologies (which are not always recognized for what they are) is rapidly increasing, and that subversion . . . must be counted as one of the primary threats to democracy in Britain today'. A corollary of that, to him, is that 'while tolerance is one of the signal virtues of a free society, it can also prove to be a crippling weakness if it is not always remembered that totalitarian movements should be tolerated only *on sufferance* [his italics] – that is, if they spread their wings too far, they will need to be clipped'.

As for the fourth principal proposition, the reader must hope that it is of no immediate relevance to British political life, since Mr Moss sets out to distinguish between two possible successors to a democratic society that had broken down irretrievably – *authoritarian* rule, which he defines as the substitution of the authority of a self-appointed or hereditary élite for the political process, with no direct interference in many areas of social, intellectual and economic life, and *totalitarian* rule in which politics and the ruling ideology intrude upon everything. To the reader, it appears that the first is regarded as by far the lesser of two evils.

With these propositions as a background, Mr Moss sets out two observations about contemporary Britain which are by no means a monopoly of the NAFF or its directors. First, he speaks of 'the extraordinary power that is concentrated in the hands of a single social pressure group, the industrial trade unions'. So do many others. Where the Moss view leaves the mainstream of British political thought is where he goes on to write of 'the disproportionate influence of communists and others who are openly dedicated to the overthrow of the free society within the British trade union movement – and by the special links between that movement and the Labour Party'.

His second observation about the British polity is equally unremarkable. He notes the 'exceptional power that is vested in a single political assembly, the House of Commons'. Mr Moss has a point here. In most other democracies there is either a clear separation of powers between those who make the laws and those who carry them out, or a sharing of power between one House of Parliament and another. There is often a Supreme Court, and usually a written constitution. Britain has none of these, and the movement in favour of acquiring such constitutional safeguards has adherents in all political parties, and among politicians of all views, save those who hope that a state based on their own particular philosophy will one day be imposed by the all-powerful House of Commons. Such people exist on both sides of the political spectrum: it is not only socialists who oppose constitutional reform on the ground that it is in essence counter-revolutionary, but it is also Conservatives like Mrs Margaret Thatcher who hope for absolute one-party control of the Commons as a means of implementing an anti-socialist crusade. The Tory leader has for long stood out as a determined opponent of electoral reform and as someone less than enthusiastic about the devolution of political power to Scotland and Wales.

This necessarily brief account of Mr Moss's thinking is intended to show that the ideas behind NAFF have some coherence. The organization has been careful to dissociate itself from the anti-black parties, and to decline the formal support of some of the outer fringe groups that sprang up in 1975 looking very like 'private armies'. It has tried hard to present itself as the vigorous element within a broad stream of opinion, even if it has had bitter quarrels with people inside the Conservative Party like Mr James Prior, who seems to regard conciliation of trade unions as one of the highest virtues, and whose

73

pandering to the notion of a closed shop upset many members of his own party.

Yet when one looks at the list of names on the Council of the NAFF it appears to be a collection of quixotic individuals who might be expected to turn a blind eye on the social progress of the twentieth century, the better to savour the political maxims of the nineteenth. The Chairman is the Lord De L'Isle, VC, KG. The members include Dr Rhodes Boyson, MP, John Braine, the young Winston Churchill, MP, Michael Ivens, director of Aims for Freedom and Enterprise, Sir Robert Thompson, KBE, CMG, DSO, MC, a specialist in 'counter-insurgency', and the eccentric Sunday newspaper writer, Peregrine Worsthorne. It is essentially a collection of outsiders.

Does this matter? Some of the things the NAFF campaigns for might be popular: they support de-nationalization of industry; strong private sectors in health and education; abolition of the closed shop; a Bill of Rights; the interests of the self-employed and the small businessman; a general campaign of resistance to 'collectivism' and trade union power. Much of this, although by no means all of it, is in tune with the conservative intellectual tide that it is fashionable to discern in other countries in Western Europe. Some of the items – opposition to the closed shop, support for the private sector of the economy, support for a Bill of Rights – are in tune with what the writer of this book has argued in columns in the *Financial Times* for some years, well before the NAFF came into existence, and in an earlier book advocating electoral reform.*

Yet in spite of all this the NAFF arouses a feeling of deep unease. It is not a group with which one would want to associate oneself. Its adherents may believe most sincerely that they seek freedom for individuals of all classes, but its apparent absence of understanding of what advances by the trade unions and the 'collectivists' have meant to those who are not wealthy or powerful is an indication of political insensitivity. Not all supporters of NAFF are rich, but any defence of individual freedom, and particularly 'economic freedom', by people of

---

* *Parliament for the People: a Handbook of Electoral Reform*, London, Temple Smith, 1976.

apparent affluence, that is couched in terms that show little feeling for what it can be like to be really poor and in need of collective support, is not only unpleasant, it can lead to attitudes that in the end must arouse the very forces of outraged revolution that these people fear so greatly. Because of its own short-sightedness, the NAFF is itself a threat to freedom.

Ideology aside, the tactics of the NAFF are, shall we say, idiosyncratic. A most revealing account of the first time a McWhirter appealed to the book of rules is in *Ross*,* the book by Norris McWhirter about his life with his twin brother, who was shot by two gunmen on the evening of 27 November 1975. The McWhirters' writings were well known. But *Ross* tells of another aspect of the twins' approach to life. It was 1947, and the pair had returned from active naval service to Trinity College, Oxford. Norris read economics under the late Anthony Crosland, the Labour Party intellectual who was Foreign Secretary when he died in February 1977.

'After a few days of close study of the university regulations,' he writes, 'I told Mr Crosland I would be going down that December. He expressed surprise . . .' Norris explained that he could get a degree in three terms. Patiently Mr Crosland explained that it could not possibly be permissible to acquire a degree in so short a time.

'In return I presented him with a single typed sheet quoting chapter and verse for our contention that if every war service dispensation was applied I was eligible, assuming I passed the examination, to graduate as a Bachelor of Arts by December. Mr Crosland looked at the sheet with some disbelief and confined himself to the comment that while possibly this was correct according to the letter of the regulations, it certainly did not comply with their spirit.

But it was Ross who took the lead in using the courts as a means of rectifying what the twins regarded as injustices. In 1954 they asked the Town Clerk of Holborn to write their names on the electoral roll as occupiers of business premises in the area. This was not usually done. They proved it was their

* Norris McWhirter, *Ross*, London, 1976.

right under the then state of law and won their suit. On the same issue Ross later sued the Home Secretary, R. A. Butler, and lost the case – but won the disclosure of some documents previously withheld by officials. Norris won a case for libel and slander against the then chairman of the London Central branch of the National Union of Journalists, of which he was a freelance member, but this was hardly in the same genre. In 1967 there was a running battle in the courts over a plan by the Borough of Enfield in London to turn thirty selective secondary schools into sixteen 'comprehensives'. Ross was so successful in these cases that, Norris recalls, at one point the late Iain MacLeod telephoned to say he ought to stop as he was in danger of alienating the middle ground. 'Ross said that he believed that when resisting doctrinaires and autocrats one had to pursue matters *à outrance*.'

And so the cases went on: over a voting recount in 1968; over the delay in 1969 by Mr James Callaghan, then Home Secretary, in implementing the recommendations of the boundary commissions that settle the outlines of constituencies before Parliamentary elections; over the television authorities' broadcasting a subliminal message in a Labour Party political broadcast, in 1970; over the proposed broadcast of what was described in the *News of the World* as an 'offensive' film, in 1973. Finally, in 1975, there was an action to require the release of cars held on the ferry, *Eagle*, by a seamen's picket line. The car-owner supported by Ross won. 'A curious feature of the case,' writes Norris, 'was that it was difficult to determine whether it was the defendant company or the defendant members of the union who were the more irritated at the intervention and humanity of the law. The fare-paying passengers had been treated like pawns . . .'

The founders of NAFF had not always agreed with Ross's tactics, but they determined to continue his legal initiatives. The major part played by the NAFF in its legal actions following Post Office 'blacking' of mail is described in Chapter 12. Its existence as a ginger group was undoubtedly a factor in increasing the anxieties of the trade union movement during the development of the Grunwick dispute.

It also grew into a force within the Conservative Party. It supported Mrs Margaret Thatcher, not Mr Edward Heath, although it would be exaggerating its influence to say that that alone led to her displacement of the previous leader of the Party. What it has done is touch certain chords within conservative hearts. Its publicity following two cases in 1976 – supporting British Rail workers expelled for not joining the union (a case that could reach the European Court of Human Rights) and Tameside parents in another famous case over comprehensive schools – brought a number of new members, and apparently resulted in the acquisition of sufficient funds to produce its newspaper *Free Nation*. It was also able to carry out its court actions, advertise, and fund a small staff. Its future is not predictable, but it could become to the Conservatives what the Tribune Group is to the Labour Party, or it could, like so many predecessors, fade away. The Grunwick case has been the biggest test of the strength of the ideas it represents for many years: both sides knew this very well, all along.

The attraction, and the danger, for the Conservatives can best be illustrated by two small pieces of evidence. The Conservative *Monthly News* of August 1977, looking very like earlier issues of the *Free Nation,* had as its main banner headline 'THE MOB RULERS', and began 'night after night this summer we have been treated on our TV screens to the nauseating spectacle of policemen being punched, kicked and injured by a bullying crowd of thugs . . .' Inside, Sir Keith Joseph wrote under the headline ' "Moderates" behind whom Red Fascism spreads' that 'Shirley Williams, Fred Mulley and Denis Howell . . . joined the Grunwick pickets'.

'These front-benchers are the frontpersons, the façade behind which the assaults on our liberties continue and behind which Red Fascism spreads.' The language may be strong, but the obvious temptation for the Tories was to tar the entire Labour movement with the brush of the 'violence on the picket-line' that people believed in because, after all, it was on television.

The evidence that there is a danger comes from an anecdote about the night on which sympathizers, including members of

77

the NAFF, helped clear the mailbags which had piled up at Grunwick because postmen refused to move them (see Chapter 12). The people who came along to rescue the mail on the Saturday night and Sunday morning of 10–11 July 1977 were, according to an eye-witness, mainly 'City types', the kind whose earlier incarnations so joyously drove buses in the General Strike. They wore jeans, but the social attitudes, as they passed the bags from hand to hand, were unmistakable. When some of the mail arrived in country outposts, ready to be forwarded to post offices where the post men were not holding up Grunwick mail, it was carried in loose-boxes.

A picture like this, of upper-class jollity on one side of the class war trenches, could do the Conservatives no good at all. A close association with the NAFF carries with it the danger that such a vision might be planted in the minds of some of the voters. The Grunwick dispute also brought out some of the internal divisions on the subject of the trade unions that persist within the Conservative Party. Mr James Prior said on 30 March 1977 that he hoped that the ACAS report recommending recognition of APEX by Grunwick would be 'heeded'; on 25 August he spoke in favour of a 'solution based on the Scarman Inquiry's recommendations'. But on 1 September Sir Keith Joseph, doubtless echoing the thoughts of a different group within the party, vigorously attacked the report and its principal recommendation, that the strikers should be reinstated. Fortunately for the Tories, however, it was the image unfavourable to Labour that people saw on their television screens in midsummer 1977.

7 The media – and the police

Nothing enters the British national consciousness until it has appeared on television, and when it does we usually get it wrong. It was, of course, the mass picketing that turned the Grunwick dispute into a national farce with tragic overtones, and so those who would blame what followed on bias or distortion by 'the media' are at least half wrong: no mass action, no coverage. If it is said that what appeared on the screen did not present a complete picture of a somewhat complicated issue, then the answer must be that it is very nearly impossible for television, with its need to present moving pictures and to restrict its reports to short sharp bursts, to get such matters right. The central point of each day's action on the streets was that trade unionists were trying by force of numbers to prevent workers they called 'scabs' from entering the factory. Television could make this plain enough. The ensuing shoving matches between some of the massed demonstrators and the sorely tried police could also be shown, but it was apparently not possible, in the nightly commentaries, to remind viewers of the causes of the dispute.

'The London Programme', broadcast late on Sunday nights by London Weekend Television, did carry a full account of the causes on 12 June 1977, immediately before the first day of mass picketing, and indeed it put out two further broadcasts, one on 26 June and one on 3 July that between them gave a full airing of the views of both sides. Apart from that, however, both newspapers and TV paid little attention to the issue before 13 June (always excepting the Communist and far-left papers).

On Thursday, 19 May, TV viewers saw the unusual sight of three Cabinet Ministers talking to Asian workers in a picket line not previously much heard of. The three were Mr Denis

Howell, Minister for Sports and President of APEX; Mrs Shirley Williams, Secretary of State for Education; and Mr Fred Mulley, Secretary of State for Defence. All three are sponsored members of APEX, and at the time they appeared the picket was relatively small and certainly peaceful. When it subsequently became associated with violent clashes with the police some grey heads in the Labour Party wondered how such a right-wing trio with such apparently impeccable social-democrat credentials could have allowed themselves to become embroiled in a dispute of that kind; the less kindly Conservative response was noted in the last chapter.

It was, however, the events of 13 June that really put the Grunwick affair on TV. The coverage by Independent Television News in the fortnight after that date amounted to nearly two hours (113 minutes 50 seconds to be precise), which is about a third of all the 'News at Ten' broadcasting time available in two weeks, and rather more if advertisement time is excluded. The BBC was similarly attentive. Of 290 minutes of BBC 'Nine O'Clock News' (including the weekend equivalent) forty minutes were devoted to Grunwick in all its aspects. Either TV is a totally ineffective means of conveying information, or such a solid pounding of the public consciousness must have a powerful effect.

There are several theories that purport to explain why this particular mass picket should have attracted so much attention. In Brent it is put about that it was the result of a tactical error by the police, who made eighty-four arrests on that first day and thus drew in far greater numbers of sympathizers to the picket lines. There is something in this theory. After 13 June, it became a matter of some urgency for well-known people who wished to show solidarity with the left wing of the Labour movement to make an appearance. The effect was even more dramatic when there were arrests. This happened to such well-known trade unionists as the Marxist Mr Arthur Scargill of the National Union of Mineworkers and such relatively little-known MPs as Mrs Audrey Wise, Labour MP for Coventry South-West. And provocative left-wingers anxious to get into fights seized the opportunity to do so.

A useful 'Who was Who' of that picket line can be compiled from the columns of the Communist *Morning Star*, and filled out from other accounts. Such a compilation might start with Mr Norman Atkinson, Labour MP for Tottenham, just behind Miss Pat Arrowsmith, peace campaigner or Mrs Regina Fischer, mother of world chess champion Bobby Fischer. Also there were such important personages as Mr Geoffrey Drain, General Secretary of the National Association of Local Government Officers, Mr Alan Fisher, General Secretary of the National Union of Public Employees, and Mr Hugh Scanlon, President of the AUEW, plus several other trade union leaders. If this balances right and left, the list of MPs present is well weighted towards the left. There were oddities: Mr Scanlon had only a few years previously breached an APEX picket line and APEX members had crossed a miners' picket (see Chapter 4). Many lunatic fringe groups and political parties joined the fray; an opportunity to have one's poster flashed on the TV in such circumstances, at no cost, is no more to be missed than an opportunity to advertise cigarettes at a football match, at high cost. At the same time many young trade unionists from London offices of newspapers, staff rooms at London schools, and others touched either by the Brent connection or by what they had seen on TV came to show sympathy and support.

Much of this, the Brent theory goes, was a chain-reaction set off by the eighty-four arrests on that first day (half of those arrested, according to the official organ of the Police Federation, being members of an ultra-left fringe group).

Perhaps there is something in that theory, but those who propagate it frequently put forward arguments that cast doubt on the wisdom or self-restraint of the police. Another theory, which is at least as plausible, is that the Grunwick site, just outside Dollis Hill underground station, is very easy to reach. Anyone willing to get up early enough in the morning could be on the picket line by seven o'clock, shout slogans at the company bus as it arrived within the following hour or so, and be on the way to a job somewhere else in London before nine. TV cameramen could be back at the studios well before noon, even if after nine there was an hour or so of scuffling on the pavements. There was plenty of time to select and edit the most dramatic film for that night's viewing. A similar event in a less accessible place would surely have received less publicity.

Once the coverage began, it developed into pure theatre, with a momentum of its own. The impression that must have been gained from continuous viewing of the TV news was of angry crowds trying to prevent the bus-load of workers reaching the gate, and policemen, sometimes patient, sometimes rough, pushing the crowds back so that the buses could get through. To Brent and the strike committee they had a smash-hit on their hands; the APEX decisions to let it run a further week, and then to organize a very large demonstration for 11 July, were taken while the fervour was still mounting. The farce was magnified when Mr Arthur Scargill and busloads of miners came down to the picket line; the Brent connection had made excellent contact with Mr Scargill's own organization.

For the Government and the trade union movement, however, the whole thing turned sour when on the morning of Friday, 24 June, the front pages of all the newspapers confirmed what people had learned from the TV the previous night; thirty-year-old constable Trevor Wilson, of the Special Patrol Group, had been knocked down by a milk bottle. The picture of him lying bleeding in the street became for many people a symbol of the Grunwick dispute quite different from the symbol of Mrs Desai standing patiently outside the factory gate. It was a nasty experience for the young constable, and it set the tone for the anti-left, anti-union comment that followed.

Was it fair? There have been many complaints from the trade union side against the behaviour of the police, and accusations that people were pulled along by the hair, or handled roughly when arrested, or treated badly while under arrest. Statements about some of these accusations are in the possession of the TUC; in other cases it did appear from the TV film that groups of policemen were piling on top of individual demonstrators, or that people were being dragged along. The general TV coverage, it is argued, did not show enough 'police brutality', and instead showed the police as martyrs.

It is not possible to say whether these accusations were true on any given day; they were certainly not true all the time. On Monday, 11 July, the day of the mass demonstration and picket, for example, the Labour movement made strenuous efforts to ensure that there would be a quiet demonstration of solidarity which would be made manifest by the orderly assembly of delegations of trade unionists from all parts of the country in a morning session of peaceful picketing to be followed by a mass march through the wastes of Willesden and a period of standing around in the hot sun listening to rousing speeches. For a large part of the morning it looked as if they would succeed. By 6.30 a.m. the pickets were lined along the pavement on both sides of the street everywhere except immediately outside the gates at Dollis Hill, where the police suited their tactics to the terrain and kept the gate side neutral by establishing it as the press area.

Shoulder to shoulder the constables, with here and there a lady constable, stood along the kerb with their backs to the chanting crowd, as between them token delegations of trade unionists (the full divisions were kept elsewhere) were allowed to march with their banners. It was the kind of interlude, half-joyous, half-menacing, that one experiences at the rough end of a football stadium.

Many copied the Italian and Portuguese Communist slogans as seen on TV: all shook their fists in unison and chanted:

> 'The workers
> United
> Shall never be defeated.'

A determined believer in the Red conspiracy might note the Marxist splinter-party banners near those who uttered this chant most often and draw a chilling conclusion; if one observed how young the faces were, and how rare was the thin, pale, unsmiling profile of the true fanatic it might be possible to take a more relaxed view.

In any event, the other songs showed little sense of subservience to putative leaders of a crusade towards a new Marxist society. Broad grins followed the announcement that Mr Arthur Scargill was present; then the ditty:

'Arthur Scargill
Walks on water
La la la la la la la.'

It was in an effort to catch this spirit and calm everyone down that no less a figure than the Assistant General Secretary of the TUC, Mr N. D. Willis, acting during the absence of Mr Len Murray on holiday, took up the megaphone and announced that he was going to sing a little song. The crowd quietened down as Mr Willis, who is not in any way emaciated, gave them three long verses of:

'I am the man
The very fat man
Wot waters the workers' beer.'

Short of producing Mr Jones and Mr Scanlon in a buskers' neck-undulating version of 'A Cairo Nightclub', this seemed about as far as the TUC could go in its efforts to keep the peace.

Mr Willis's courage is all the more to be commended for his once having been told by Mr Michael Foot that the only man who sings 'Wot waters the workers' beer' worse than he does is the Chancellor of the Exchequer.

But in spite of the good humour, and the efforts of the many important trade union leaders present, the nasty undertone did break out.

It is probably only in Britain that unarmed police will stand still and keep smiling as the crowds they are seeking to control sing a verse whose punchline is 'And shit on the coppers below.'

Another observer of the picket line, present on many other days, writes:

There was considerable violence and viciousness but probably not as bad as impressions of it left by newspapers and TV. There was a lot of pushing and shoving, considerable struggling by many who were arrested; there were fights between individual officers and individual pickets, and several instances of running battles involving large numbers of police and pickets over a seventy-five-yard stretch of road, both in Chapter Road and Copper Road. In a number of instances individual policemen, isolated from the rest of their colleagues were beaten and kicked by groups of pickets while police-men were on the ground. There was not much blood spilt however, except when the policeman was bottled. When it happened an official picket who was shouting at the crowd through a loudhailer that they were a disgrace to the trade union movement was laughed at and jeered.

There were a number of dubious cases where police appeared to use more force than necessary, once when a girl was being taken to an SPG van by three policemen when somehow her head made contact with the van bonnet. The fighting was messy and confused as in all 'riots'. A picket says he saw this or that policeman do some-thing when in fact to all the reporters standing by it just looked like a general punch-up.

The bottling of a policeman outside pubs on a Saturday night is not an uncommon occurrence; it hardly warrants one paragraph in a local paper. One senior police officer said 'You should go into the terraces at Arsenal sometimes. It makes this look chicken feed.'

There was a confusing police policy on the number of pickets al-lowed on the gate. This was eventually agreed with APEX at half a dozen but before that and sometimes after the agreement the police allowed more pickets to stand at the gate only to change their minds and tell the pickets to move on. Sometimes they refused and the police pushed or pulled them away. The police tactics of contain-ment, pushing back and 'crowding' pickets often went on several minutes after violence ended. There were complaints from pickets that they were being crushed.

There was a great deal of provocation dished out to the police. During arrests there was a crescendo of abuse, including shouts like 'you racist fucking scum' and 'you fascist pigs' directed at no officer in particular. After violence individual policemen were picked out for abuse. On one occasion (among many) an officer was harangued by two pickets with things like 'you bastard fucking shit'. The officer just turned away.

The pickets were deliberately trying to stop the buses. Violence almost always started as the pickets pushed and heaved forward against the police line to 'get at' the bus. They often refused to get on the pavement when told to. This simple disobedience often led to individual confrontations.

This account can presumably be matched by accounts from individual pickets who have complained of the way in which they were treated by the police. Several such complaints have been listened to while collecting material for this chapter, and there is no doubt that on the strikers' and pickets' side there is a widespread feeling that the police were not impartial (their job in upholding the law was to let the bus carrying the non-striking workers to the factory through the gates) and that many of them were very rough or very brutal.

As reported in the *Financial Times* of 22 June 1976, for example, Mr Ian Mikardo, the left-wing Labour MP for Bethnal Green and Bow, said that the scenes at the picket lines had been reminiscent of the Mosley marches of the 1930s.

'Such violence that occurred was not from the action of the pickets or those who had come to show solidarity with them', he claimed.

Mr Mikardo said that some 'rent-a-crowd' elements had been present, but the majority on the picket lines were 'decent trade unionists, shop stewards and trade council members'.

'At no time did I see any violence offered to the police or any provocation other than verbal provocation.' But, he alleged, police had pushed into the crowd to drag certain people out. 'One woman who protested was dragged by her hair into the police bus. Audrey Wise protested and the police said to her: "You'll do instead".'

Mr Mikardo claimed that the bus taking employees into the plant had been used 'like a projectile' to break through the picket line. 'The bus came round a corner. It came very fast, and accelerated as it reached the area where most of the people were. It was deliberately used as a projectile, as a tank.

'It mowed through everything, up to the gate and through ... Everyone fell back from the bus except one poor chap who was knocked down. It was the worst piece of intimidation I have seen anywhere. If anyone had driven their car like that bus was driven, they would have been rightly charged. It was absolutely incredible.'

Mr Mikardo said that the MPs had demanded an explanation from the Home Secretary, Mr Rees, about the use of plain-clothes police, 'heavily disguised ... in casual clothes'. Another MP, Mr Ron Thomas (Labour, Bristol NW), said: 'I have never seen such violence as that used this morning. One youth was dragged for yards. I don't know how his neck wasn't broken. It was purely fortuitous that many more people were not injured by the bus. It was a clear case of dangerous and reckless driving.' These statements by politicians are typical of the most extreme allegations. The writer had a trip on the bus, and found it peaceful and well driven.

The police can, and did lose their tempers, and it would be foolish to deny that numbers of them probably did so in the mêlées that broke out when the crowd surged forward and threatened to take over one particular strategic point or another. Some of them may have been deliberately provocative, or too free with arrests, or especially rough. Anyone who has been under arrest or locked in a cell, as the writer has been, will know that it is not a pleasant experience and that once you are regarded as a 'villain' the police can be far from gentle. But they took hard knocks. No one knows how many cuts and bruises, or sore heads, or similar hurts the demonstrators suffered. The Home Secretary told the House of Commons on 14 July that in the previous four weeks there had been 377 arrests and 243 policemen had been injured.

These things do matter; what perhaps matters more is to get into clear focus the violence that did occur. This was a British argument involving hot tempers, flying fists, and the occasional missile, such as a milk bottle.

There was no evidence of an organized use of weapons, or hard projectiles, by the pickets; the police had not by July 1977 drawn even their short batons. If this is far from the worst that could happen in British terms it is even further from what might happen in cities where bricks are thrown and fire-hoses repulse the rioters, or where the weapons are knives and guns. On both sides, pickets and police, what actually took place was less threatening than the rhetoric used to describe it.

The TV, and the subsequent headlines in the newspapers, may have made matters worse for the trade union movement by fitting in with this inflated rhetoric, so that the emotional force of the picture put in people's heads, a picture of 'violence on the streets', was probably increased by the necessarily artificial message of film and big black type. These certainly exaggerated what was happening but they did not falsify the basic truth.

Yet because of the rhetoric, feelings on both sides became unnecessarily strong. Many trade unionists on the left insist that the police were simply the tools of the capitalists at Grunwick; dark hints about what was believed to be a close relationship between the constabulary and the management there were heard everywhere. Some attempt was made to appeal to brotherhood between working-class policemen and working-class pickets; the common shout was 'What about when you cops want to strike for a pay rise?' – and one sharp reply from the constables was 'it wouldn't take us forty weeks'. But the hostility and the suspicion built up, and it spilt over to 'the media' as well as the police in general.

This came out in several ways. On 26 June production of the *Observer* was held up for several hours and some 250,000 copies were lost when print workers objected to an advertisement placed by the National Association for Freedom headed 'UNION PRIVATE ARMIES HAVE NO PLACE HERE.' On 1 July, two officials of the National Graphical Association objected to a leading article in the *Sun*. Because of an admitted ambiguity a change in the wording was made but it was subsequently found that a line of type had been removed. The paper was published with a blank space instead of the leader, and some of the printers refused to handle the typescript that would have given an explanation. There must have been second thoughts, however, because the next day the leader was published in full.

In a later comment the Press Council deprecated 'these blatant and inexcusable instances of press censorship which constitute a grave danger to the freedom of the press as, indeed, the National Graphical Association machine minders' chapel (office branch) at the *Observer* seems to have recognized after the stoppage had occurred'.

Some print workers and office staff from Fleet Street went down to the picket lines at Grunwick even though the newspapers they worked for wrote in disapproval of the mass picket. Thus the emotional force of the national, televised dispute was felt far away from the place where it all began. This manifestation of British class conflict also affected the television news services. Complaints were made by various people against both ITN and the BBC, but accusations of bias in the editing of film for TV are never easy to substantiate. In the case of the BBC the newscaster, Miss Angela Rippon, was reported to have used the phrase 'trade unionists and other extremists' on the 'Nine O'Clock News', this was regarded by some people as evidence of a serious anti-union bias at the BBC. In fact the full phrase was 'the union wants to distinguish between trade unionists, and other extremists which it feels are responsible for the violence' – a simple case of sloppy writing. Such matters must be largely impressionistic; the best judgement of the TV coverage is probably that it was inevitably superficial, but that that is in the nature of the medium, not the result of bias.

If the left felt strongly about the police and the TV (and, of course, in an event whose quality was altered when it became a nightly serial story the two were intermixed in many minds), the police were more angry about the left and the demonstrators than an impartial force should allow itself to be. At one level there were those who wondered why there had not been a baton-charge; at another there were the powerful feelings contained in the columns of *Police*, the monthly magazine of the Police Federation. The July 1977 issue had a photograph of a fallen constable, obviously in pain; as a caption the journal reprinted protests against police 'brutality' from the Liverpool, Merseyside and Greenwich Trades Councils. The juxtaposition told very clearly what the police thought of those Councils.

When it comes to the British passions aroused by street conflicts, individual policemen are just as affected as everyone else, however impassive their faces may look beneath the oval helmets on TV. The people whose heads may roll, however, are higher up in the Cabinet, and at the Trades Union Congress.

8 The Government – and the TUC

It was the fuss in the newspapers and on television following the mass picketing and demonstrations of mid-June 1977 that really alerted the Cabinet and its fellow-power, the General Council of the TUC, to the dangers of the Grunwick affair. Prior to that it was regarded as a fairly insignificant industrial dispute. It was, perhaps, a difficult one, since the company was more stubborn than anybody expected. There was a particular embarrassment early in November 1976 when the Union of Post Office Workers gave its blessing to the refusal by some of its members to handle Grunwick mail, but that died down fairly quickly, although it flared up in June 1977 when the Cricklewood postmen voted in favour of blacking the company's mail once again. This early difficulty aside, the long-simmering dispute rarely penetrated the consciousness of anyone of importance until the week beginning 13 June 1977.

Throughout those nine months of gestation the attitude of the Government and the TUC seemed to be 'here is a recalcitrant employer; he must be brought to heel', but afterwards, when the disturbances on the streets had had their effect on public opinion, it changed to 'we must cool this one down before it overwhelms us'. The change between these two attitudes is in itself a comment on the fragility of our institutions; one is reminded of the relentlessly detailed description by Alexis de Tocqueville of how a similar internal rotting away during the period of the *ancien régime* led inexorably to the revolution of 1789, although right at the very last moment, even when it was under way, no one realized what was happening, or why.

From the Government's point of view Grunwick was a minor Department of Employment responsibility for most of the first nine months, except for the brief flare-up at the Post Office when the Attorney-General and the Department of Industry (as the department responsible for the PO) came into it. To the TUC it was mainly a matter of registering the due proportion of shock and horror at what Mr Grantham was telling them, while keeping a close watch on the related dispute over an abortive postal workers' boycott of South African mail. To appreciate the change in tone once the tele-drama of the picket lines began, one must start by noting this earlier, quieter, attitude.

Mr Grantham first brought the dispute to the official attention of the TUC in a speech at its 108th annual congress in Brighton on the morning of 7 September, just eighteen days after Devshi Bhudia had walked out of the mail-order department in Chapter Road.

'What we want,' he said, 'is support from the whole of the trade union movement to denounce this kind of employer and to see that people who are disadvantaged, people who are seeking the basic rights that all of us expect, have the full support of the trade union movement . . .' He was able to announce that he had already won a pledge of full support from Mr Tom Jackson of the Union of Post Office Workers, and that the Transport and General Workers' Union was seeking to organize the drivers at Grunwick.

The moral tone of Mr Grantham's appeal was set by his choice of the debate on 'racialism' as the opportunity for his speech. The context suggested that he was primarily interested in helping racially oppressed employees. This is a matter on which TUC statements of principle are usually of the loftiest, although not all black workers on the shop floor would testify to the brotherliness of the attitudes of the white fellow-workers.

The quasi-independent Advisory, Conciliation and Arbitration Service, ACAS, first offered its services to the company on 31 August, eleven days after the walk-out; in this way the official administrative machinery was set to work, in low gear at first. The news that a difficult case existed spread upwards to the Department of Employment and even, in at least one paper, to Downing Street, but at that early stage it was merely noted. If anyone at that highest level thought about it at all, the thought was quickly set aside on the ground that the Department of

Employment, plus APEX, the TUC, and ACAS would soon bring about a solution.

By the end of September Mr Grantham was so certain that even the formidable force of these institutions acting in concert would not bring an early resolution that he decided to take personal charge of the case, a remarkable decision for a busy General Secretary of a union as large as APEX. His mounting sense that this would be a major event in trade union history led him to start knocking on doors and tugging on sleeves. On 23 September Mr Reg Freeson, Labour MP for Brent East, wrote to the company, asking it to reconsider. On 5 October Mr Grantham asked the Secretary of State for Employment, Mr Albert Booth, to set up a Court of Inquiry into the dispute; the reply was that the new laws passed under the social contract, including the Employment Protection Act, should first be given a chance to work.

As the report of Lord Scarman's Commission of Inquiry – set up, after much disturbance, eight months later – notes, Mr Grantham 'accepted the suggestion (with some misgivings, which subsequent events may seem to have justified) that the union should refer a recognition issue to ACAS'. The minister responsible was plainly confident at the time that the powers already in existence and ranged against the company would work, even though when he had received his first reports on Grunwick, in September, he had felt instinctively that this was going to be an awkward one. But he went over it with his officials, and the upshot was that his department, which was slowly bringing the provisions of the Employment Protection Act into operation, was loth to prejudice the chances of ACAS. Mr Booth had talked about the case to the chairman of ACAS, Mr Jim Mortimer; he was very cooperative and assured the Minister that somehow there would be a survey of what was happening at Grunwick. In the event, Mr Mortimer later told Mr Booth, it was a shock to ACAS to find out how difficult that would be.

Thus when, on 15 October, Mr Grantham formally asked ACAS to recommend that the company recognize APEX, the Secretary of State for Employment was already involved. When

APEX also decided to try and win a ruling on unfair dismissal from an industrial tribunal it was done following a discussion between Mr Grantham and Mr Booth about the difficulty of getting such a ruling where there is no discrimination against particular employees (see Chapter 11).

And when, early in October, Mr Grantham wrote to the TUC asking for help, he was simply acting to stimulate forces that had already been alerted, not least by the Brent Trades Council. Mr Len Murray, the General Secretary of the TUC, responded by sending a circular letter, no. 27, dated 7 October 1976, requesting unions to 'give all possible assistance to APEX, including asking their members not to use the services of the company'.

The machinery ticked on. ACAS began its long attempt to win the willing cooperation of Grunwick (see Chapter 11) and at a meeting of the Finance and General Purposes Committee of the TUC on 25 October it was decided that something serious should be done about bringing pressure to bear on the company. The General Secretary of the Union of Post Office Workers, Mr Tom Jackson, told the committee at that meeting (Minute no. 16) that he had little doubt that action by the UPW would have a profound effect, and that the proposal would be discussed by his executive. It was agreed that Mr Murray and Mr Jackson should discuss what to do next.

Officially the forthcoming blacking of Grunwick mail was not thought to be illegal. It did not occur to anyone inside the Department of Employment, or apparently in the other departments involved, that a secondary boycott, or a sympathy strike, by post office workers was against the law. When the blacking started on 1 November the unpaid public relations consultant for Grunwick, Mr John Gorst, MP, put down a Private Notice question for the Secretary of State for Employment; it was taken the next day. The question was not on that day regarded as of sufficient importance to warrant a reply from Mr Booth himself; it was answered by Mr Harold Walker, Minister of State at Mr Booth's department. This junior Minister said: 'I am sure that the General Secretary of the Union of Post Office Workers is quite familiar with the law in this respect. It is not for me to judge the legality or illegality of such action.'

Even at that stage, it will be seen, it was felt that the machine, ACAS and APEX, reinforced by the postal blacking, would surely now do the work and bring the company into line. This was not an unreasonable opinion; Mr George Ward himself had said that cutting off the mail service was like cutting the jugular vein of Grunwick. Indeed on the first day of the blacking, before Mr Walker spoke, Grunwick had told ACAS that it would cooperate in the inquiry if ACAS could get the blacking stopped.

As it turned out the blacking was called off on 4 November, when the National Association for Freedom asked the High Court for an injunction against the Post Office and the union. According to the Scarman report, the reason for the UPW undertaking not to interfere with the mail was that the union relied upon what ACAS had told them about the intentions of the company, 'and upon an assurance given by the company that it would cooperate in the inquiry'. Just what assurances were given, if any, were the subject of conflicting accounts by ACAS and spokesmen for Grunwick later on; there is no precise information on this point.

Seen from the Department of Employment, that seemed to be that. There had been a full debate in Parliament on 4 November, called under the emergency rule by the Conservatives. The Secretary of State himself had spoken, the Labour side had managed to put across many allegations about conditions of employment at Grunwick while the Conservatives had managed to pursue their arguments about the rule of law. It was a tiresome little dust-up, but the company would surely see sense now and cooperate with APEX. The noise of the machinery died down to an almost complacent hum.

It was much the same at the TUC. Certainly, growls were heard from the postmen as ACAS found that it could not overcome the objections of Grunwick to the proposed procedure for ascertaining the opinions of the workforce. The delay was regarded as deliberate prevarication, and the machine rumbled. The postmen threatened to renew their blacking. Mr Len Murray came down to Willesden to address a meeting organized by the strike committee and the Brent Trades Council; he identified himself and the TUC completely with the strikers' cause. But that was all. By and large, ACAS was left to get on with it as best it could, and when the service decided just before Christmas to ballot the strikers since the company would not provide names and addresses of those still in their employ the opinion was that everyone had best await the ACAS report.

An apparently different, but in fact related, issue attracted rather more attention. In January 1977 the Union of Post Office Workers declared that it would support an international boycott of postal and telecommunications services to South Africa, with consequences described more fully in Chapter 12. The NAFF took the UPW and the Post Office Engineering Union to court, after failing to persuade the Attorney-General, Mr Sam Silkin, to start proceedings.

The first legal skirmish, in the High Court, was lost by Mr John Gouriet, the administrative director of NAFF, but the second, in the Appeal Court, was won. In July, the House of Lords reversed this judgement again, but early in 1977 the state of the law deeply troubled the TUC. Minute No. 46 of the meeting of its Finance and General Purposes Committee, on 21 February, tells why. First, the committee was told, following the Appeal Court decision the law in effect restricted, perhaps even abolished, the right of employees of the Post Office to 'take industrial action'. The Prime Minister had advised the two affected unions, the UPW and the UPOE, to discuss the necessary changes in the law with the Secretary of State for Industry.

To the TUC this may have seemed merely troublesome; what appeared to be even more serious was that the case might have created a new kind of civil action against which trade unions had no immunity, not even under the Labour Government's new legislation of 1974 to 1976, the prime purpose of which had been to free trade unions from the restraints of the law. The effect, the committee was informed, was that cases could be brought against trade unionists and unions in a variety of circumstances. For example, a private individual might charge pickets with obstruction, or start an action against workers who were in breach of a bye-law at, say, an airport. Even worse, the

Appeal Court decision could be the foundation of what the TUC feared would be 'substantial further encroachment by judges into trade union immunities'. The new doctrine might even be extended to cases of unlawful conduct involving a breach of contract or, say, an action alleging that damages (a 'tort' in legal language) had been suffered by some third party. This was a challenge to trade union power that had to be met. After a protracted discussion – would the courts not express their traditional antipathy for the unions anyway? would the Labour Attorney-General's case not be damaged by a trade union appeal? – it was agreed that the TUC should support the post office unions in their appeal to the House of Lords.

In the minds of the leaders of the new Establishment, the TUC and the Labour Government, this case was closely associated with the post office workers' blacking of mail from Grunwick the previous November, and the same connection was made when the blacking started again, on 15 June 1977, without the official blessing of the UPW. Such action was by then known to be illegal. The unions had been assured in May that the necessary legislation amending the Post Office and Telegraph Acts would be introduced 'as soon as possible', but with Labour unable to command an overall majority for such measures in Parliament that might be a long way ahead.

For the first half of 1977 this issue was regarded by the TUC and the Ministers involved as of greater importance than the long dispute in Willesden. Everything changed after 13 June. The alarm bells rang, and as the struggles on the picket line became more intense, they rang louder and longer. The machinery started to move into top gear. All at once Grunwick became a Home Office responsibility, because of the police; a major Department of Employment concern, because it was a labour dispute; a matter for the Attorney-General, because it was in the courts as well as on the streets; and a case for the Secretary of State for Industry, because he answered for the Post Office. At Downing Street the Prime Minister was quick to see that this was a danger for the Labour Government, since it had to keep the peace, which meant supporting the police against the demonstrators, while at the same time it had to maintain the goodwill of the trade unions, on whose behalf the demonstrations were taking place. So for a few weeks in June the daily consultations on Grunwick, a photographic company employing a few hundred people in Willesden, occupied more time in the Prime Minister's office than any other industrial matter in the history of the post-1974 Labour Government save, perhaps, the troubles of the giant British Leyland motor company after it was nationalized.

On 19 May, before the troubles started, the Prime Minister, Mr James Callaghan, had had a brief foretaste of what was to come when two of his Cabinet Ministers, Mrs Shirley Williams and Mr Fred Mulley, along with the Minister for Sport, Mr Denis Howell, had been photographed on the then peaceful picket line. A private, unconfirmed, report suggests that he subsequently told his Ministers not to go down to the line again without consulting him first. But he was just as much taken by surprise as everyone else when the mass picket, originally called for one week only, led to what the Scarman report later called 'unacceptable social strife'. At the very beginning he told two of the Ministers obviously most directly concerned, Mr Booth at Employment and Mr Silkin, Attorney-General, to get moving. The Home Office automatically came in because the police arrested eighty-four pickets on the first day and all kinds of people began to telephone the Home Secretary, including many Labour MPs. Mr Callaghan could not leave it at that; the matter was too important, too dangerous for his Government.

He asked his close political associate and friend, the Home Secretary, to chair a special *ad hoc* Cabinet committee to oversee the day-to-day handling of the dispute. It is not unusual to establish a committee of this kind to meet a crisis; in the case of Grunwick the crisis seemed so pressing that after 21 June Mr Rees's committee met nearly every day, and sometimes twice a day, mostly in his room at the House of Commons. (This is an imposing chamber, guarded by an outer office. The occupant immediately before Mr Rees was the Leader of the Opposition, Mrs Thatcher.) The meetings were usually attended by Mr Rees, Mr Booth, Mr Silkin, and, as the post office blacking developed, Mr Varley. Civil servants were brought in, and full reports were taken to Downing Street every day; what is not likely to be found in any future official record is an account of any direct, private conversations between the Prime Minister and Mr Rees. An early meeting was held by the PM in his own room.

The Home Secretary's first task was to establish whether the tactics adopted by the new Commissioner for Metropolitan Police, Mr David McNee, were reasonable. The trade unionists associated with the mass picket, their MP friends, and others were complaining loudly of 'police brutality'. At the same time conservatives in all parties were wondering whether the police could not have done more to contain the crowds. On 22 June the Conservatives issued a statement, signed by Mrs Margaret Thatcher, calling on the Prime Minister to 'state categorically' that the police had the full backing and support of the Government. In the early days of the dispute there was some questioning inside the Home Office of the McNee policies. It was not really until a fortnight after the start of the picketing, when Mr Rees himself went down to visit Grunwick that he saw for himself that the tactics adopted were dictated by the terrain. In those narrow streets there was no option but to press the crowds back on the pavements, if the bus carrying the willing workers was to be given its legal right to pass. Those who protested about 'brutality' were informed of the new police complaints procedures just coming into use. Even MPs like Mrs Audrey Wise, who was much shaken by her arrest, were heard sympathetically, but told much the same thing. The placating of its own left-wing MPs became a serious preoccupation of this essentially right-wing Labour Government's senior Ministers.

While Mr Rees was fighting his own particular fires, Mr Booth, spurred by the urgent words from Downing Street, tried to arrange a settlement. This was his first attempt to bring the parties together. Previously, the Government had been content to let the forces ranged against Mr Ward and his company do their work; now, with the disorder on the picket line bringing Labour into disrepute, an effort to bring about a discreet settlement would have to be made. It is worth looking at this part of the history in some detail, because it shows something of the character of the opponent who was standing out against the new Establishment, a man who dared to insist that he need not accept any pressure from anyone and that his only obligation was to obey the law. In so acting, Mr George Ward was of course advised by others, including the NAFF (an interested party with its own ideology to consider), and Mr John Gorst, MP, as well as his own lawyers. Yet anyone who has heard him out at length will see that, at bottom, he was standing by his own beliefs as best he could. Let us start this small tale at the very beginning.

On Saturday 18 June officials at the Department of Employment were faced with a problem. Following instructions from their Secretary of State, they had invited Mr Grantham for APEX and Mr Mortimer for ACAS to meet Mr Booth at the Department's offices in St James's Square. This was easy enough; the difficulty arose when they tried to pass on the third invitation, which was addressed to Mr George Ward. They could not find him. His factory was closed for the weekend, and it appeared that his telephone number was not listed. It was frustrating. Then someone had an idea. He telephoned a senior official at the Home Office. That official telephoned someone at Scotland Yard, who in turn telephoned the local police. They finally ran down the quarry. At 7 p.m. on that Saturday evening Mr Ward telephoned Mr Booth's Private Secretary at his home. The vital contact was made at last. Mr Booth's invitation was passed on, and the Department had Mr Ward's home telephone number.

It did not, however, have an acceptance. Mr Ward said he would need to consult his colleagues. He could not come while the factory was under siege; it was scarcely possible for him to leave and he did not wish to take part in discussions under duress. The recent appearance on the picket line of Government Ministers had made matters worse. Anyway, what did Mr Booth want to talk about?

Exactly twenty-four hours later, at seven o'clock on the evening of Sunday 19 June, the private secretary tried again. Mr Booth would be willing to meet Mr Ward separately, before any joint discussions with APEX. Perhaps a police car could bring him through the picket lines. Mr Ward said he would need to consult his advisers, then read out a letter he was sending to Mr Booth by hand the following morning, in which he suggested meeting Mr Booth at Grunwick. 'He can come and see me. He has greater freedom of movement,' said Mr Ward. Deadlock. Try again, said the Minister the following day. There was much else to do that day. Mr Booth met Mr Grantham and Mr Mortimer. There was action on the picket line, a brief debate in the House, and an important meeting of the Finance and General Purposes Committee of the TUC. All this news flowed in. At twenty to five that afternoon the private secretary telephoned the company and asked for Mr Ward. He was in a meeting, said the lady who answered. He would ring back. Twenty minutes later the determined official called again. This time he managed to get through to Mr K. Pearson, a director of the company. The official tried to allay the fears of the board of Grunwick. Mr Booth had an open mind; he would be happy to discuss an agenda as a first step in the discussions.

At half past five Mr Ward himself phoned back. Mr Booth should come out to Grunwick to show he was not afraid, he said. He related an anecdote, which he said indicated the bias of Government Ministers against him. Perhaps Mr Booth could address further invitations in writing; he, Mr Ward, was a formal man and thought this would aid rational and logical discussion. Perhaps Mr Booth could indicate just how he felt he could help. A quarter of an hour later he phoned the official again, this time to complain that the BBC had reported Mr Booth as saying that Mr Ward had refused a meeting; the reply was that Mr Booth had made no such comment. An effort would be made to clear up any misunderstanding.

At seven o'clock on that busy Monday evening the private secretary rang back to read out the draft of a letter from Mr Booth, putting the invitation in writing as requested. According to Mr Booth, Mr Ward said yes, provided that the meeting was kept confidential. Ten minutes later the private secretary phoned again, to ask whether by any chance Mr Ward would come in that evening. The managing director of Grunwick replied, reasonably enough for the time of day, that he was tired and hungry and would make contact again in the morning when he had received the letter from Mr Booth.

He did. On 21 June, in a letter delivered by hand, he wrote to Mr Booth:

Dear Mr Booth,

I have received a letter from your Private Secretary Mr Emmot, dated 20 June, in which he reiterates your desire for a meeting with me and notes that I expressed the view yesterday that a meeting should not necessarily take place at Grunwick.

Since receiving your Private Secretary's letter, my attention has been drawn to a report in today's *Times* Parliamentary report in which the Home Secretary is quoted in the House of Commons as saying 'None of my colleagues are unbiased about the law, but there may be some of us who are in a different situation when it comes to the working conditions in the factory.'

I have also noted the statement of Mr Eric Heffer, an ex-Labour Minister, who is quoted as referring to '... those workers who have been working for poor wages, in rotten conditions under a rotten boss, who by any standards is still living in the last century'.

In view of these opinions, I must insist that no meaningful talks can take place until the biased and totally unfounded impressions have been completely eradicated from the mind of you and your Cabinet colleagues. The only way for this to be done is for you to see for yourself at Grunwick that there is no truth in the allegations. Only after you have done this could it be possible for other matters unrelated to the High Court proceedings to be discussed.

I remain available to meet you at Grunwick at any time convenient to you.

Yours Sincerely,
George Ward
Managing Director, Grunwick Processing Laboratories.

That same day the Secretary of State replied:

Dear Mr Ward,

I have received your letter of 21 June. As you know, my Private Secretary has had a number of telephone conversations with you on my behalf during the last three days, in an effort to persuade you to come and talk to me about the dispute. You were widely reported in

101

the press as having declined my invitation and as having said that you saw no point in a discussion. I subsequently received a letter from you to this effect.

Yesterday you told my Secretary that you were prepared to come provided that the meeting was private. You asked for a letter confirming these arrangements and received that letter by hand last night.

You now say that you will not come, and explain this change because of certain views expressed in Parliament yesterday. You will appreciate that this is a matter of major public concern which, subject only to the Speaker's rulings, is one on which all MPs are entitled to express their views in the House. I can only draw the conclusion that you have no intention of accepting my invitation but I would urge you once again to reconsider. My invitation remains open, and I believe that it would be in the interests of all concerned that you should now accept it.

You will appreciate that I am being pressed in Parliament to seek ways of opening discussions and resolving this protracted dispute, and that I am answerable to Parliament as to why this has so far proved impossible.

Since you have published your letter without informing me in advance, and contrary to my understanding of how you wished to proceed, I have no alternative but to publish this reply.

Yours sincerely,
Albert Booth.

If we had no other evidence in the case, these two letters alone would be enough to show the unbridgeable gulf between the new Establishment and its challenger. But there is an abundance of other evidence.

The following evening, at twenty to seven, Mr Ward telephoned the Department of Employment and apologized for not having replied sooner to a letter from the private secretary sent that morning and asking him to come later in the day to meet the Secretary of State. He had been seeing his legal advisers. With them, he could come to St James's Square the following day. He suggested 2 or 2.15 p.m. He and the private secretary then haggled about the time, but after Mr Ward started talking about Friday, they agreed on three o'clock. The meeting was on the strict understanding that nobody from APEX or ACAS would be present. At eleven that night Mr Ward telephoned the private secretary at home. He confirmed the appointment for the following day. And so after five days, with crowds creating havoc outside his factory gates, with exchanges in Parliament and elsewhere daily reported in the newspapers, with the TUC gearing up to act against him, and with the Secretary of State for Employment having his officials telephone, telephone, and telephone again, Mr Ward agreed to come and talk.

We will return to consider these talks in a moment but first it must be noted that Mr Booth's efforts at mediation, strenuous as they were, were but one part of the mighty effort of the Government to bring peace in the streets. It was not even the part of the operation in which Mr Booth's colleagues placed most faith; to the committee under Mr Rees the first step was to reduce the amount of picketing and bring it under control. To most of the other protagonists a second step, with the same object in view, was to appoint a special Court of Inquiry in the hope that everyone would go home while it deliberated. The Department of Employment was not wholly satisfied with that approach. Its speciality is mediation; a Court of Inquiry seemed like a distraction and in any case it should not be used except as a last resort. In the past, in more deferential years, the sight of a distinguished judge or other prominent person sifting the facts with patience and integrity would usually be enough to calm people down; this time no one could be certain of the result. If a Court of Inquiry is used too often, then like any other weapon of public opinion, its force might be weakened. Mr Booth, who would have to appoint such a Court, was in no hurry to do so.

Yet the pressures were increasing every day. The Government was very worried. A letter from Mr Grantham to Mr Len Murray dated 17 June had announced the continuation of the mass picketing the following week, and asked for full support from the General Council of the TUC. He had that very day asked Mr Booth to establish a Court of Inquiry (thus repeating his original request of the previous October) and he looked to the TUC to make representations to the Government about this, as well as to call on member unions to support the struggle. This letter was debated by the Finance and General Purposes Committee of the TUC on Monday 20 June and again by the

General Council itself on the following Wednesday. At that Council meeting Mr Hugh Scanlon, the President of the Amalgamated Union of Engineering Workers, was heard to utter the important sentence, 'this is a matter of principle', a sentence that, in such a forum, could only mean that the TUC could hardly allow APEX to lose. A statement issued by the General Council offered the support asked for by APEX, but in cautious terms, speaking of 'financial and practical aid to those on strike' and effectively dodging the issue of mass picketing. The week beginning Monday 20 June opened with 1,200 pickets on the line at the peak period in the morning, and continued with the arrest of Mrs Wise on the Tuesday and, on the Thursday, the arrest of Mr Arthur Scargill, at the head of a contingent of miners. Worst of all from every point of view, was the day on which PC Trevor Wilson was knocked down by a flying bottle. The Government and TUC recognized that this event was particularly damaging for the Labour movement as a whole.

It is hardly surprising, therefore, that the use of a Court of Inquiry was put forward at meetings of the Rees committee from the very beginning. At the first meeting on 21 June the most urgent item on the agenda was the Prime Minister's request that a means be found of limiting the number of pickets, and that ways be found of taking the heat out of the dispute. A Court of Inquiry was one way, but Mr Booth was still trying mediation; if he could get both sides to accept a mediator that would be better. Meanwhile there were other possibilities. A meeting between Mr Grantham and Scotland Yard was arranged. The Attorney-General spoke of making an application to bring forward the High Court hearing of the case between Grunwick and ACAS; the next day ACAS did this successfully, but it did not seem to be enough.

On 23 June the sub-committee heard that the Commissioner of Police had reported that Scotland Yard was finding that the troubles outside Grunwick were giving the Metropolitan Police greater difficulty than any mass picket in their experience. It seemed to be getting out of hand. APEX seemed unable to control it. Mr Grantham was not accustomed to the kind of event his union had helped to create. His visit to the Yard did not at that stage lead to much confidence among Ministers, but later the picket line did gradually come under some kind of control. Meanwhile the use of armbands by pickets was suggested, an idea with which the Prime Minister managed to have himself associated in the newspapers.

The next day they debated other possibilities. The assembled ministers heard through Mr Rees that although the Commissioner of Police may have certain powers to close roads or railway stations, he was reluctant to use them. Clearing the streets around the factory would only move the point of confrontation, possibly to less convenient areas. More hopefully, Mr Booth reported that the TUC's cautiously worded statement of the previous day had been designed to help dissuade miners from coming down in too large numbers to join the picket line. (If so, it was not very effective.)

Thus it can be seen that during this week the great TUC–Government machine turned away from the previous mood of confidence in its own powers, and towards making peace, so that those powers themselves would not be threatened. Public statements, and pronouncements in Parliament, were peppered with references to the misfortunes of the strikers and the recalcitrance of the company, but in reality the first preoccupation of the new Establishment was the same as that of the old conservative one in similar circumstances: order must be restored. The difference is that the chosen method was not based primarily on asserting the rule of law, but rather on manipulating an uneasy balance between the use of police power (unpopular among unions and in the party) and the use of powers of compromise, of persuasion, of mollification, of appeasement.

It was at this point in the development of the Government–TUC approach that Mr Ward came to St James's Square, accompanied by one of his directors, a legal adviser, and Mr John Gorst, MP. The date was 23 June. Sitting for the Government were Mr Booth, the Director of Information at the Ministry, and an under-secretary, Mr Matt Wake, who had in earlier days been posted to ACAS when it was first set up. Mr Gorst started by reviewing the history of the dispute. The issue of union recognition was before the courts. It would be solved in the courts. There could be no reinstatement of those who had been sacked, under any circumstances. Allegations that terms and conditions at the factory were intolerable were absurd. Meanwhile, could the Secretary of State do something about the intimidatory pickets, and the hampering of mail? Mr Booth, in reply, said he had been asked by APEX to set up a court of inquiry, but was reluctant to do so. At that stage, said Mr Gorst, while the High Court hearing was still on its way, a court of inquiry would be regarded by the firm as an intervention in the due process of law. Was the suggestion being made merely because of the mass pickets? Mr Ward tried hard even at this meeting to get Mr Booth to visit the factory; he also insisted, several times, that his company wanted only to exercise its legal rights and that it would therefore be bound only by the findings of the courts. The gulf remained as wide as ever.

That weekend, at Chequers, the little group of ministers under Mr Rees met again, with Mr Callaghan himself taking the chair. The Prime Minister was getting agitated. Mr Silkin, who had been present at an Anglo-American seminar on 'The News and the Law' at Hythe (Lord Justice Scarman was also there), had been called away to Chequers on the Saturday afternoon. There had to be action on all fronts. Through the TUC and UPW the postmen had to be persuaded to return to work; the Post Office must also be contacted. Booth could continue to try mediation, if only to show reasonableness. But the desirability of setting up a court of inquiry should now be given urgent consideration. The message from Mr Callaghan was plain.

To go through the details of Mr Booth's further attempts at mediation would be superfluous; the above account of contacts between Mr Ward and his advisers on the one side and the Department on the other gives the flavour of the matter. To Mr Ward, his actions were self-defence; to the Department they smacked of prevarication. There was a statement from Booth and a counter-statement from Ward on Sunday night; a meeting on Monday failed to result in any meaningful agreement on the terms for accepting mediation. It is not necessary to rehearse the arguments of both sides at that meeting; all along Mr Ward was saying, in essence, that he would abide by what the law told him, and no more, while Mr Booth was saying that the law itself was not a sufficient mechanism for the maintenance of good industrial relations and that extra-legal mediation was essential. They could not agree.

Thus in that week the other ministers crowded in on the Secretary for Employment and, armed with the Prime Minister's hints of Sunday, pressed forward to a court of inquiry. There was to be an emergency debate in the Commons on the thirtieth; this seemed like a good target date. The Rees subcommittee called for an official paper to be prepared. On the twenty-eighth they debated it. Mr Booth was reluctant to the end. A court of inquiry was the last shot in the locker. It was not satisfactory if the parties to the dispute would not be bound by the outcome. Its powers were limited; its recommendations did not have legal force and even its ability to subpoena witnesses was in doubt.

But there was an overwhelming desire to move the action off the streets. The postal dispute was growing, and there was some fear that there might be a national strike by postmen if the Post Office carried out its threat to send home men who would not handle Grunwick mail. Mr Silkin was uneasy about this; he had for some time been under attack for not taking legal action against the postmen. His interests, like those of the Home Secretary, whose police were struggling on the line, would be best served by a quick announcement of a court of inquiry. The next day Mr Booth, whose departmental interests were different, conceded that mediation was dead.

He met Mr Grantham at noon and told him that he was under pressure from some of his colleagues to set up an urgent court of inquiry as a means of restoring law and order. At 5.30 he met Mr Tom Jackson who said it was unlikely that the appointment of a court of inquiry would make any difference to the attitude of UPW members who were not handling Grunwick mail. They would not return to normal work until there was some realistic prospect of resolving the dispute. But that day's

107

meeting of the Rees committee decided that the court should be announced the following day. Its terms of reference were discussed, and it was agreed that Lord Justice Scarman should be the chairman. Mr J. P. Lowry, director of personnel at British Leyland (now a nationalized industry) and a former director of the Engineering Employers' Federation, would be a member. So would Mr Terence Parry, General Secretary of the Fire Brigades Union, and a member of the General Council of the TUC. At 8.00 that evening Mr Grantham led an APEX delegation to St James's Square, where the possible effect of a court of inquiry was discussed. Mr Grantham suggested waiting a little longer. But the decision was already made.

At the beginning it was not certain that the court would have its intended effect, but in fact it did cool tempers on the picket line and the only serious flare-up after that was on 11 July, the 'national day of action', whose mood is described in the preceding chapter. Meanwhile, everyone would have to wait. There was no person on the Court of Inquiry representing the views of Mr Ward or Mr Gorst or the NAFF. The new Establishment could draw a deep breath.

Thus the first objective of the Government–TUC machine was met. The struggle was moved off the streets, where it was difficult to control, into courtrooms. Nobody seemed to be bothered with the obvious question, which was that if those who took to the streets were thus confirmed in their view that that was the only way to get results, the seeds were being sown for worse confrontations later. This was not the way matters are seen by the new Establishment; its mind is not absolutely clear about the rule of law. What was clear at the end of June was that there was now a need for a few victories for the trade union and Labour Party side, to offset the devastating defeat, in public opinion terms, of the televised drama of the picket lines.

One such victory came on 12 July, when the High Court ruled in favour of ACAS. The next day APEX, responding to the continued pressure from the Government and the TUC to make certain that the dreadful scenes of June would not be repeated, persuaded its strike committee to agree that there would be no further demonstrations, marches, or large-scale picketing while the Court of Inquiry was deliberating. The TUC circularized this statement, in a further attempt to bring the militant supporters of the Grunwick strikers under control.

At this point the tide seemed to turn the wrong way from the point of view of the new Establishment's clients. Grunwick ran a surprise secret ballot at the factory, after which Gallup reported that 85 per cent of the willing workers were against any form of trade union representation. The Post Office allowed the firm to retrieve sixty-five mailbags from Cricklewood. And on 29 July, later named 'Black Friday' by the militants, the Appeal Court reversed the earlier High Court judgement and came out against ACAS and for Grunwick. On the same day the postmen at Cricklewood agreed, following much pressure from their own union (allegedly including a threat to withhold their strike pay) to end the blacking of Grunwick mail. APEX, still receiving earnest persuasion from the Government and the TUC instructed its own strike committee, after heated debate, to call off a mass picket originally scheduled for 8 August. (It was held anyway, but on a reduced scale and in much muted form.)

The new Establishment itself was not ruffled. It had relative peace on the streets, which was its first requisite, and it had regained its confidence that in the end its side would win the war, even if a few battles were lost. On 26 July Mr Silkin won his appeal in the House of Lords, in the case of Gouriet v. the Post Office Unions, thus setting aside some of the fears that had so concerned the TUC about further judicial intervention in trade union affairs. ACAS decided to go to the Lords for a final verdict in its dispute with Grunwick. During August the underlying divisions between the militant strike committee and the Brent Trades Council on the one side and APEX, backed by the Government and the TUC on the other, became more marked; the machine was confident that its own methods would prevail. On the twenty-fifth the Scarman Court produced its report, which supported the claim of the strikers for reinstatement and by spreading blame for civil disorder more or less equally between all sides gave the new Establishment the public relations advantage it had hoped for all along. Yet, it remained an open question whether the dispute would be solved in that way, or whether there would be a new upsurge of street fighting or illegal 'blacking' of a kind that a Labour Government could not welcome in the run-up to a General Election, even if the weight of blame could be shifted to the other side. The gulf remained unbridgeable. It is at this stage that we must ask, why?

9   The class conflict

The answer is that Britain is still two nations. The class conflict continues; a farce like the one at Grunwick is a wonderful opportunity, some would say too good to miss, for 'us' to jerk the knee into the groin and the boot into the face of 'them'. This perception of the country as one in which there is still bitter class conflict may not commend itself to everyone. The contrary view is that such unpleasantness is mostly a thing of the past and that anyway a great many working-class adults vote Conservative. Yet to appreciate why the Grunwick dispute could become so explosive so quickly one must consider the evidence in support of the assertion that Disraeli's two nations have not yet been united.

It is to be found in every social statistic published by the Government. For example, the number of people who feel that they suffer from a limiting, long-standing illness rises as you go down the scale of social classes. The lower your social class the younger you are likely to die. The higher your social class the better your child is likely to do at school.

Between 7 and 8 out of every thousand babies born to mothers in Social Class I in Scotland are stillborn; for Social Class V, the lowest, the figure is between sixteen and seventeen stillbirths per thousand (1973 figures). All over Britain, at the top everyone gets paid in full when off sick; at the bottom there is still great reliance on state sickness benefit. Absence from work due to illness or accidents is three times as common among manual workers as among those who practise a profession. Lower-class women have their babies younger than higher-class women. Just about everything else, from the newspapers we read through the food we eat to the holiday we take is differentiated by class.

111

Even cigarette smoking is graded according to social class: the lower down the scale, the more people smoke. An excellent summary of the numerous relevant statistical series is to be found in the 1975 edition of the Central Statistical Office annual, *Social Trends*, pages 10 to 29. The concluding comment by the CSO is that 'we have ... shown that social class differences still exist in all areas of concern in Great Britain; and that, in the few cases where we do have trend data, such differences do not seem to be much less important than in earlier decades'.

This is not the same thing as saying that there is still great poverty and hardship, in the pre-1939 sense of the words, in modern Britain. Everyone is of course considerably better off, as the figures for income, housing, car ownership, ownership of refrigerators, possession of TV sets and telephones and all the other indicators of affluence demonstrate; the point is that the old inequalities persist, so that in spite of a great deal of movement between the classes, it is probably still true that many people feel themselves to be members of the working class, skilled or manual, on a weekly wage for life.

Of course not all such people are Marxists, or adherents of the far left, or even supporters of the Labour Party. The evidence of successive general elections is that many working-class voters may stay at home to let a Labour Government fall, or even go out to vote for the Conservatives. When they turn on the TV and see the police battling with strikers outside Grunwick, they are as likely to wonder what the country is coming to as are middle-class TV viewers. (How many TV viewers, in any social class, identified their own interests with those of the essentially petit bourgeois Asians who were so divided among themselves at Grunwick must remain a mystery.)

Yet when all these complicating factors have been allowed for, the social and economic divisions between the classes remain, and it is on this basis that most trade union and business leaders argue. It is here that the class conflict can turn rough. Once certain trade union sensibilities were touched, the need to defeat Grunwick and its allies became almost overpowering, just as those who opposed the trade unions believed that a defeat for the company would be a defeat for British democracy.

This rising in the blood of class instinct can only be understood as a matter of emotion; there is not a great deal of reason in the Grunwick story. If we were ruled by reason the company might have found a way of alleviating the grievances of its workers long before the dispute erupted. Once it did break out, leaders of a trade union for whom reason was the only guide might have kept their patience until the long-drawn-out proceedings in the courts produced a verdict, even if that meant providing perhaps a little more income support for those who were on strike and seeking redress. The remedies available through the law and existing institutions are imperfect and in some cases uncertain (see Chapter 11), but they are better remedies, more generously geared to the demands of trade unions and the needs of workers than anything offered in Britain before. As will be seen, if the law as written could not help the Grunwick strikers, the omissions are primarily the fault of the trade union movement. Unfortunately, the trade union movement eventually let its sense of outrage lead it to take the case to the streets, in a determined effort to ensure that it would not be seen to lose,

It would be foolish to suppose that reason alone can guide the way people behave. As Lord Justice Scarman assured Mr Jack Dromey at a difficult moment in the Court of Inquiry hearing on the afternoon of Monday 18 July: 'There is nothing wrong with emotion. It is just as important as intellect.' But the Grunwick farce took this one further. Emotion became more powerful than reason. How much these opposing passions were strongly felt by the people who expressed them, and how much they were postures, is hard to judge, but there were moments during the early summer of 1977 when it seemed as if the whole affair was fairly well divorced from reality. People simply took up positions.

The leading position on the trade union side is called 'solidarity'. This is a word that cannot easily be defined, because its connotations seem endless. In its purest form it means the linking of trade union members in a brotherly, and nowadays sisterly, attempt to defeat enemies of the moment. Trade Union power is based on the ability of the members to organize themselves, or be organized, in such a way that their collective force becomes overwhelming.

But 'solidarity' can also mean one union fighting another for members. It can mean the organization of the rank and file in an effort to throw out the officials. It can mean putting someone out of work because he or she is not a union member, or obliging everyone to come out on strike when many of them do not really want to. It can also mean some trade unionists – coal-miners, say – using their power to acquire a larger share of the national wealth at the expense of fellow trade unionists who have less power at their command. In its best sense, 'solidarity' is the coming together of people who are willing to struggle on behalf of their own or others' lives, even if in the course of the struggle many of those out on strike, or on the picket lines, suffer some loss and hardship.

In its worst sense 'solidarity' means brusquely asserting the power of an organization, be it a branch, a national headquarters of a trade union, or the TUC itself. This authority is exerted over others, be they individuals, groups of other workers, companies, or Parliament itself. During the Grunwick dispute the posture adopted by many of the trade unions was that of solidarity in its best sense. They presumably meant this sincerely, but the reality is that for much of the time the movement simply could not stomach the possibility of defeat, so that it was willing to use to excess the power at its disposal.

This does not justify the posture adopted by some of the trade union movement's opponents, who seemed to take the view that the unions' principal demand, which was for a chance to represent the interests of the disaffected Grunwick workers, had no merit. To stand simply on the provisions of the law while pushing aside any consideration of common decency, or legitimate grievances, or the genuine wish of employees or recently disaffected employees to belong to a trade union presents the worst side of those who believe that the 'rule of law' is an essential safeguard of freedom. As a company, Grunwick could not be called generous; its behaviour during the dispute was 'unreasonable when judged by the norms of good industrial

114

relations practice' says the Scarman report It was a hard case. If, even so, one is to argue that trade unions over-reacted, it is important to start by noting this.

For it is possible to accept both the fundamental rights of trade unions, as free associations of working people, while yet insisting on the importance of the rule of law. The trouble is that the class conflict makes this difficult, since many trade unionists approach the equation backwards, their eyes fixed on the painful history of their movement. They look back to the riots and violence that followed the repeal of the Combination Laws of 1824; to the six Tolpuddle Martyrs, farm labourers who were transported to Australia for taking secret oaths to join a union; to the arrest and imprisonment of the Chartists; to continuing setbacks as the courts reversed gains supposedly made; to their defeat in the General Strike of 1926; and to attempts by Parliament, especially in the nineteenth century, to keep them in check at a time when the balance of power was lopsidedly in favour of the employers.

Those who subscribe to the doctrine that in spite of all this the rule of law is a fundamental protection of all our freedoms, including the freedoms of trade union members, do so on the ground that if certain groups live within an extra-legal world of their own, no one is safe.

For example, in the second, 1919, edition of his *Law and Public Opinion in England*, A. V. Dicey condemned the 1906 Trade Disputes Act, which released trade unions, their members and their officials, from the possibility of being sued by aggrieved parties for civil wrongs, such as libel. Section 4 of that Act, wrote Dicey,

confers upon a trade union a freedom from civil liability for the commission of even the most heinous wrong by the union or its servants, and in short confers upon every trade union a privilege and protection not possessed by any other person or body of persons, whether corporate or unincorporate, throughout the United Kingdom.

In 1919 the results were not yet fully appreciated by the public, according to Dicey, yet, he predicted, the effect of the

Act would be to make 'a trade union a privileged body exempted from the ordinary law of the land. No such privileged body has ever before been deliberately created by an English Parliament.'

If those who have faith in the rule of law stand shoulder to shoulder with the trade unions, so that they may look backwards together, it can be seen that since 1906 the trade union movement has acquired a degree of constitutional immunity that perhaps exceeds what even Dicey feared.

This process has in recent years worked so energetically in favour of trade union power that if the Grunwick combatants, the proponents of trade union immunity and the proponents of the rule of law, turn round and face the present they must surely acknowledge that it has gone far enough – the rule of law side will naturally say too far. For a start the law itself now supports most of the legitimate aims of working people: from the old Factory Inspectorate to the modern Acts laying down reasonable terms for contracts of employment, training, dismissals, redundancy, pensions, disclosure of information, and equal pay, most employees are safeguarded by a phalanx of legislation. Some of it may be in need of improvement; for example, the Grunwick case has shown that people who walk out, and are then sacked, cannot easily win compensation from an unwilling employer or anyone else. Such defects in the law are discussed in Chapter 11. Taken as a whole, however, industrial legislation now protects people through most of their working lives.

The trade unions are the watchdogs of these protective laws; they see it as part of their duty to ensure that they are enforced, and to add to the list. Whatever they do, they currently have greater freedom to act independently of the legal system than at any time in British history.

The story of how this has come about is a long one, but its last chapter begins with the setting up in 1965 of a Royal Commission

to consider relations between managements and employees and the role of trade unions and employers' associations in promoting the interests of their members and in accelerating the social and economic advance of the nation, with particular reference to the Law affecting the activities of these bodies.'

The Commission, under the chairmanship of Lord Donovan, published its report in 1968. It said:

> With very few exceptions, the law prevents no one from joining a trade union, and protects no one against attempts made by others to impede the exercise of his freedom of association. The law has never been called upon to help in organizing or operating a system of workers' representation at enterprise or at plant level. It has done little to protect individual workers against the exercise by employers of their power of dismissal, or against the exercise by trade unions of their power of expulsion. In short, it has been the traditional policy of the law as far as possible not to intervene in the system of industrial relations.
>
> The evidence which we have received shows a wide measure of agreement that this non-intervention should continue to be the normal policy (p. 203).

Yet it proposed that statutory machinery to safeguard workers against unfair dismissal should be established. There should be protection of workers from the possible abuse of power by trade unions, although it was not suggested that closed shops should be banned. A new code of law affecting trade unions and employers' associations was proposed, as was the setting up of an Industrial Relations Commission.

In spite of its endorsement of 'non-intervention', the Donovan report created a climate of opinion in favour of bringing modern trade unions more fully within the umbrella of the general law, and that in turn created an outraged reaction from the unions themselves. The Labour Government of 1964–70, which had set up the Commission, failed to carry through such proposals following bitter opposition from the leading unions and the TUC; its Conservative successor took the logic of the arguments one step further with its far-reaching and comprehensive Industrial Relations Act of 1971. In opposition, Labour fought fiercely against provisions within that Act that it had itself proposed while in office. During those years, 1970–74, the Labour leaders convinced themselves that only a close and binding relationship with the trade unions could ensure electoral success and security while in office. Thus when the party won the two elections of 1974 it was hardly surprising that it repealed the 1971 Act and replaced it with legislation favoured, and in some cases virtually drafted, by the trade unions themselves. These new laws did not stop at a mere return to the 'non-intervention' of the Donovan report; they distinctly tilted the balance of power towards the trade union side.

There is a perfectly logical social justification for Labour's assiduous wooing of the unions during 1974 and 1975. It reads this way. In his first eighteen months of office the Conservative Prime Minister, Mr Edward Heath, had aroused all the old class antagonisms by pressing forward with a certain insensitivity with policies that seemed anti-trade union and unfair to the worse-off section of the population. About half-way through his term in mid-1972, the outrage that this created, and the growth in unemployment, led him to reverse those policies, but the emotional damage was done. To the trade unions, it was exacerbated by the existence of the Industrial Relations Act, which they regarded as a retreat from non-intervention and a tilt in the balance of power against them. They pledged themselves to defeat it, and most unions refused the cooperation that alone could make it work. When Mr Heath left office after a divisive miners' strike, which had forced the Conservative Government to declare a three-day week to conserve energy, there was a sense that the most urgent task confronting the new Labour Government was to cool the social fever. Appeasing the trade unions did seem to many in Mr Wilson's 1974 Cabinet to be an honourable way of binding up what they regarded as the social wounds of the Heath years.

The first fruit of this policy was the Trade Union and Labour Relations Act, 1974, which passed through Parliament while the minority Labour Government that took office in March of that year was working towards the subsequent election held in October. The new law repealed the Industrial Relations Act, which at once restored the immunity of trade unions from being sued – that very immunity which Dicey complained about when writing of the 1906 Trade Disputes Act, and which the Conseivatives had withdrawn. Bits of the 1971 Act favourable to working people, such as the provisions on unfair dismissal, were salvaged. Some demands made by trade unions could not be granted at that time, because the Government was in a minority and the Opposition could push its amendments through.

In that same year the Health and Safety at Work Act provided for a wide extension of the statutory protection of employees down to a requirement that company directors' annual reports must in future contain information about the health and safety arrangements within the firm.

Then in 1975 the Employment Protection Act, which seemed to some outsiders to have been drafted by the TUC, established the Advisory, Conciliation and Arbitration Service on a legal basis (it had previously been set up without legal powers). ACAS, from which there could be appeals to the newly established Central Arbitration Committee, was intended to promote collective bargaining and good industrial relations; its powers are discussed in Chapter 11. The law also concerned itself with the rights of workers to job security and guaranteed pay during lay-offs; it also gave new trade union rights to organize, to be recognized, and to obtain information from employers.

Writing in the *Industrial Law Journal* (Volume 5, page 23), Roger Benedictus, lecturer in law at the University of Leicester, commented:

In a longer perspective, the collective aspects of the Act can be viewed as a significant attempt to shift the balance of industrial power from employers to employees, thereby reflecting the TUC's considerable involvement in the preparation of this legislation. The Act indicates a striking new willingness on the part of the unions to achieve their ends by legislation rather than by collective bargaining backed up, if necessary, by industrial action. So to that extent, and whatever the success of its detailed provisions, the Employment Protection Act 1975 may well represent a watershed in British labour law.

Yet this is not all that the trade unions won from the Labour Government during those years. The Industry Act, 1975, enabled a Minister to require companies to give certain information to unions. The Trade Union and Labour Relations

(Amendment) Act, 1976, further extended the freedom of trade unions from the restraints of law that were provided in the original 1974 Act, including those items on the TUC shopping list that the minority Labour Government had not been able to deliver in 1974. Statutory requirements on union rules were withdrawn; the definition of 'trade dispute' – the phrase that tells the law to keep off – was widened to include international action against multi-national companies; the legitimacy of the closed shop was restored to its pre-1971 position, at a time when pressure for this restriction of the rights of dissenting individuals was increasing; and in several other apparently small but in fact important ways various restraints on what trade unions could do were removed.

Even this brief summary of the laws favourable to trade unions is not the whole account of their recent advance towards becoming a power in the land. The close and direct involvement of the TUC in every aspect of public life, under the name of the 'social contract', so advanced the power of the movement that, on one famous occasion, people seemed to think that the leader of the Transport and General Workers' Union, Mr Jack Jones, was more important than the Prime Minister. The effect on public opinion of trade union demonstrations of power is a central part of the Grunwick story; in the long run it is opinion that will either endorse or halt the advance of the unions. In 1968, before the TUC defeated the Labour Government's proposed new law restricting union power, about half the respondents to a National Opinion Poll survey thought that trade unions were too powerful. This figure rose to just above 60 per cent the following year, including half of the trade unionists among those questioned (*NOP Political Bulletin*, September/October 1970). It climbed steadily, according to successive polls by various organizations, until in May 1975 the Opinion Research Centre reported that three quarters of its respondents in a poll commissioned by Independent Television News thought that the trade unions should have less power.

The following year, according to a Market and Opinion Research International poll, reported in the *Economist* of 10 January, three quarters of all respondents and two thirds of trade unionists still believed that trade unions had too much power in Britain. Individual opinion polls taken just once on uncommon subjects may be suspect, and the precise percentage results should never be accepted down to the last decimal point – but the cumulative evidence of the many successive polls is overwhelming. Most people think trade unions have too much power.

Some, a very few, have decided that counter-action is necessary. A number of associations whose prime purpose seemed to be to organize resistance to trade unions sprang up in the early 1970s; one or two of them, with their threats of quasi-military tactics, could be written off as the blatherings of eccentrics. The National Association for Freedom, which was formed in 1975, could not be so easily dismissed.

The NAFF is discussed in Chapter 6; the important point about its effect on the TUC is that it came to be seen as a legal-minded counter-attack by people who sought to check the unions' power and might even wish to go further and take away some of the gains that had been made. Either way, the broader issue remains: will the trade unions be obliged to accept a prescribed place within an agreed constitution? That they should is part of the argument of this book; that when they supported street action over the Grunwick case they seemed not to have acquired the maturity that should accompany power is another part of the argument. But first let us consider the law of picketing itself.

10 The argument – picketing

The word 'picket' means different things to different people, with the result that it leads to confusion whenever there is an argument. To most people it probably means something along the lines of the *Shorter Oxford English Dictionary* definition: 'men stationed by a trade union or the like, to watch men going to work during a strike, and to endeavour to dissuade or deter them'. This has been the spirit behind the law since 1875: it has remained constant in spite of several technically important changes.

At present this common, 'respectable' meaning of the word is reflected in Section 15 of the Trade Union and Labour Relations Act of 1974, which says that

it shall be lawful for one or more persons in contemplation or furtherance of a trade dispute to attend at or near (a) a place where another person works or carries on business; or (b) any other place where another person happens to be, not being a place where he resides,* for the purpose only of peacefully obtaining or communicating information, or peacefully persuading any person to work or abstain from working.

Quite another meaning is attached to the word 'picket' by many of those who themselves stand outside factory gates. 'Whatever the law has said,' writes Stuart Weir, who stood with the Grunwick crowd, 'pickets have always tried to restrain strike-breaking workers from crossing the picket line, and are always likely to do so' (*New Society*, 30 June 1977). Some pickets, in some strikes, try to use force or threats in their efforts to 'restrain' those who are heading for the factory gates. The modern mass picket is designed to achieve the same end by sheer weight of numbers.

* The 1906 Trade Disputes Act did allow picketing of a person's home.

The conflict between these two conceptions is an excellent example of the conflict between those who place their faith in the 'rule of law' and those who see 'solidarity' as an essential weapon for trade unionists who run up against what they regard as a recalcitrant opponent. As Mr Weir puts it, 'two traditions are in conflict; the individualistic middle class tradition which believes that freedom resides only in the law; and the Labour movement's belief that working people's rights and freedoms lie in their readiness to take collective action to assert them'.

When there is a mass picket combined with a mass demonstration, the word 'picket' takes on third and fourth shades of meaning. To some middle-of-the-road trade unionists, the creation of a public commotion may be a reasonable way of showing that large numbers of ordinary, decent people, support a particular cause. To the revolutionary parties of the left, such an event is an excellent way of winning a battle in the class war. 'Oh, what a beautiful morning!' proclaimed *Socialist Worker*, organ of the Socialist Workers' Party (formerly the International Socialists), in its issue of 16 July – and it devoted its front page and three inside pages to the story of the mass picket, demonstration and march on Monday, 11 July, 'The morning the rank and file stopped Grunwick', as its front-page banner put it.

After some hours of picketing, demonstrating, and struggling on that Monday morning, the official trade union leaders present persuaded most of the crowd to join their protest march. This was intended to show that night's TV viewers that there was heavy support for the TUC, APEX, and the Grunwick strikers, and that this came from people who did not get into fights with the police, or use mob tactics to shut a factory. The *Socialist Worker* noted that drawing the crowds away to the march provided an opportunity for the 'scabs' bus' to get through, and commented:

The lesson will not be lost on many of those taking part in mass action for the first time. Rank and file action can swiftly transform working-class hopes and aspirations into reality – but only if a clear break is made with the indecision of the present trade union leadership.

Picketing outside Grunwick was 'respectable' enough at first. British tradition allows the police to interpret the 1974 law according to local circumstance. They might say that six pickets are enough for peaceful persuasion, and that any others will be arrested for obstructing the highway. Such police interpretations are not always accepted by the courts: six Grunwick pickets convicted of obstruction in February 1976 appealed against the verdict and won, with costs awarded against the police. In most everyday strikes, however, the local chief constable's arrangements are usually observed by both sides.

The picketing outside Grunwick was kept more or less peaceful by these methods throughout the long simmering that began on 20 August 1976 and did not come to the boil until 13 June 1977, the first day of the mass demonstrations. There were minor disputes, and scenes of confusion, and accusations that the police often changed their minds about the informal arrangements, but there was no great outrage. The unwritten rules worked, if imperfectly. Most of that time, as the tiny band of Asian ladies and their slowly growing number of supporters stood outside the factory gates, in bitter cold, in pouring rain, or simply under bleak grey skies, there were plenty of opportunities for peaceful persuasion – for those who were not on strike had to walk past the pickets. Shouts of 'Scab!' or 'Blackleg!', or, no doubt, the Gujerati equivalent of 'the dung of thy mother is the least malodorous part of her anatomy' may not sound particularly persuasive to the disinterested outsider, but they are common enough on any picket line and little is done about it unless one of the constables standing nearby decides that that kind of language is a threat to the peace.

No serious affront to established opinion can be read into that part of the story. The trouble comes when pickets, perhaps frustrated by the failure of peaceful persuasion, decide that the unwritten rules about the relationship between a small number of dissatisfied workers and the police might be a good enough way of keeping the peace, but that they are of little use as a means of winning the argument. This was what moved the Grunwick strike committee, the Brent Trades and Labour Council, and, eventually, APEX itself when its executive committee decided in May that a mass picket must be called.

It is useful to be clear about this. There is no convincing evidence that when the official call for support went out those involved anticipated the result. They might have hoped for large numbers of supporters, to show solidarity, and some of them no doubt banked on the weight of numbers as a means of making the continuation of work at the factory impossible. But the scenes of confusion, shoving, thumping, and an apparent breakdown of general law and order in the area around Dollis Hill underground station were probably not generally expected. If they had been, APEX might have drawn back: after all it was those scenes, shown every night on television, that so turned public opinion against the trade union side of the argument.

Perhaps they should have known better. At the sitting of the Court of Inquiry on 14 July, Lord Justice Scarman asked Mr Grantham 'What in your view is the industrial justification for a mass picket?' Carefully distinguishing between what APEX had envisaged and what actually happened, the General Secretary of APEX replied:

'The industrial justification for the kind of picket that we asked for on the original day was, first of all, to impress upon the people inside that we were concerned about the fact that this issue was going on for a long time and, secondly, to draw the attention of the public authorities to the fact that we had a strike that had been running then for over forty weeks, which we had attempted to resolve by all the legitimate available means to us and upon which there was no prospect of making any progress unless somebody came along and said "This is an issue that has to be resolved".'

Questioned further, Mr Grantham replied: 'The law deals with certain situations, it does not deal with this situation where the other side to the problem is not prepared ever to meet you or seek to resolve the issues. The law is written on the assumption that it is dealing with reasonable human beings who will settle their own problems.'

Lord Justice Scarman pressed his point; Mr Grantham's answers lengthened. Eventually there was this exchange:

Scarman: 'I see your dilemma, Mr Grantham, but let me put

125

to you as starkly as I can what I think the problem was in front of your Executive Council. Either you were going to be patient and suffer the delay and frustration of the legal process or you were going to call into existence a scene on the streets which looked very disorderly and socially as well as industrially dangerous. Faced with that, why did you choose the remedy on the streets?'

Grantham: 'The situation is that we saw the remedy of a mass picket as a peaceful mass picket ... That was our intention because we were satisfied after the most careful examination of a very long-running dispute, which was already some forty weeks old, that if we went through all the legal delays and the procedures at the end of the day, another ten months later, we could still not have got our members reinstated. With the greatest respect our members are human beings. Strikes do not go on for two years with no prospect of getting a settlement, and at some stage you either have to say that you accept that this man will get away with it or you say that you will take steps to bring home to people the realities of the situation. It was a terrible dilemma.'

Lord Justice Scarman then pointed out that in law there was no way that Grunwick could be forced to reinstate the employees it had sacked; at best, it seemed, compensation could be negotiated. While the strikers were waiting for this they were getting 'fairly ample' strike pay. To the union side it seemed that this suggestion did not take account of the difficulty of negotiating with the company. As Mr Len Gristey, the APEX official directly responsible for the day-to-day handling of the dispute, told the court that same Thursday afternoon:

'There have been very few strikes in this country which match the history of the Grunwick strike. Very few have the examples of violence on the picket line which have existed during the course of this dispute. Very few of them have the incidents of a company being able to find alternative methods of supply and thus evade the intention of the picket line ... Very few of them, frankly, have ever had a strike force composed almost entirely of immigrant labour, and that is some-

126

thing which is far more serious than it sounds simply sitting here mouthing out the words.'

Scarman: 'I think we know what you mean.'

Gristey: 'I must say, my Lord, that at the end of eleven months of such a dispute it is inevitable, when the employer continues to remain immovable, that, having tried everything else which lies within the known history of other disputes in this country, we had to look for some other methods to seek to persuade the company that really they were not on, that really they were defying the whole of trade union principle within this country and, of course, we feel somewhat proud of that trade union principle because, having fought long and hard in days long before my time to establish it, it has gone from strength to strength in very recent years . . .

'Thus, I have to say, my Lord, that it seemed to us that the only possible way in which to continue to promote the interests of our members and the other interests which, of course, now centre around the dispute was to introduce the mass picket.'

These extracts have been quoted at some length because they provide the most favourable exposition of why APEX decided to call in the crowds. To their way of thinking the change in the nature of the picket line from a small exercise in peaceful persuasion to a large, yet still peaceful, demonstration was unavoidable . . . The subsequent change to a daily mock-battle in the streets may not have been planned. Nevertheless it was very damaging: not only the ideological enemies of the trade union movement, but also many middle-of-the-road members of the Labour Party and numbers of trade unionists disapproved.

The signals of distress came from the right, to be sure; Mr Ronald Bell, the Conservative MP for Beaconsfield, told the House of Commons that 'gang warfare has taken over and challenges not only the rule of law, but democracy itself'. Yet Mr David Steel, the leader of the Liberal Party, drew the distinction between 'picketing by people who work in a place and by associated union members', on the one hand, and ' "Rent-a-mob" picketing' on the other. A Labour MP, Mr Bruce Douglass-Mann, said that though many people in his party had no sympathy whatever with Grunwick, they regarded the sort

127

of picketing that had taken place there as 'intimidation, as a threat to freedom and as almost inevitably creating the violence that took place'.

In defence the Secretary of State for Employment, Mr Albert Booth, said that 'If the calls of the TUC and APEX had been heeded by all those who took part in the demonstration there would have been no violence.' But this defence seemed lame to many. People who fear such demonstrations are presumably saying to themselves, consciously or otherwise, that this is where the modern growth of trade union power has to stop. The unions may win battles in Parliament, especially when there is a Labour Government, and in factories and offices other than the kind typified by Grunwick – but when their power is made manifest on the streets many are quick to announce that the whole of our democracy is threatened. 'Our laws are being disregarded right and left,' said Lord Denning, Master of the Rolls, at a public meeting on 28 June, in a strong statement for which he was subsequently rebuked by higher authority. 'The mobs are out. The police are being subjected to violence. Intimidation and violence are contrary to the law of the land. It should be condemned by every responsible citizen.' Echoing another common thought he added, 'One of the great problems of the day is not so much the power of the executive government as the power of the great groups in the land.'

Yet in this sense the Grunwick affair was nothing new.

In 1965–7 the trade unions battled continuously against a North Carolina employer, Mr Robert Pomeranz, who took the view that just as the unions had the right to withdraw their labour, so did the employer have the right to hire whomsoever he pleased. This was not acceptable to many trade unionists in Stockport, where his Roberts-Arundel factory had been taken over by his company in 1965. The dispute began with an argument over issues as small as those that set off the Grunwick firecracker (there was something about a tea break and the employment of women in the traditionally male engineering industry) and grew, like Grunwick, to the point at which it became a matter of principle, the principle of recognition, for the TUC.

During this dispute something like the 'flying pickets' of later quarrels were used, with results that sound familiar. On 23 February 1967, for example, 1,000 engineering workers drawn from the surrounding area were more than a match for the eighty policemen on duty. Some £4,000 worth of damage was done when a hail of bricks and the consequent flying glass brought work in the offices to a halt. In the end the factory was closed, the jobs it provided lost. To the trade union movement this was a draw, not a victory; if the rank and file members had visited the comfortable, mother factory in Sanford, North Carolina, and seen the women workers, busy and disciplined and without a trade union, leaving to drive to homes the Stockport workers could only dream of, in Chevrolets and Fords beyond their grasp, their view of the essential nature of trade unionism might have been modified.

'Flying pickets' – trade union members from various parts of the country gathered in one place to provide mass support in a difficult dispute – were used with marked effect during the 1972 miners' strike, when on one famous occasion the purpose was to close the Saltley coke depot. The police were caught in the crush; the lorries could not get through. Pickets of this kind were used in the 1973 building workers' strike; the trade unionists' justification was that many men on the building sites were interested only in short-term financial gain rather than the spirit of trade unionism – or, to put it another way, they saw no advantage to themselves in joining a union. Some of these individualistic workers formed anti-picket squads; there were fights at some sites. Mr Des Warren was sentenced to three years' imprisonment and Mr Eric Tomlinson to two years after being convicted of conspiring to intimidate workers. They became known as the 'Shrewsbury Two' and, to the left in the trade union movement, martyrs.

No change in the law on picketing is likely to prevent people from trying to organize mass pickets and demonstrations when they feel strongly enough about an issue; no change, that is, that could be accepted by an essentially free society. The necessary changes must make such outbursts of feeling unnecessary by providing just solutions within the law. There are, however, some changes that might make the work of the police easier.

The law might, for example, stipulate that only persons directly employed by the company, government department or local authority, involved in the row could act as pickets when there was a dispute. The number of pickets could be prescribed. If the limit was put at, say, half a dozen the police could keep the others, including any crowds that assembled, well away from the gates. It could be made obligatory for pickets to wear armbands, or it could be said that only those who were recognized by trade unions as pickets would be given the legal right to stand in protest. During the most troublesome street demonstrations outside Grunwick there was much support for ideas of this kind among Conservatives and some in the Labour Party.

Some politicians have suggested that the TUC might agree to a code of conduct limiting the number of pickets, in return for a change in the law that would provide for a right to stop lorries and buses before they enter the factory gates. The foundation of this argument is that the 1906 Act, upon which current picketing law is so closely modelled, was written before the motor age. It did not take into account the possibility of employers using buses to drive their willing workers, or strike-breakers, as the pickets would have it, through the lines. In the Grunwick case this argument does not stand up, since the buses were not introduced until the second day of the mass picketing, after nine months during which those who walked in to work were well able to hear the views of those who were on strike. It is true that the small band of women pickets could not stop lorries and vans bringing supplies to Grunwick during those long months of waiting, but to say, as some of the trade unionists did, that the mass picket was a simple response to the use of buses, is inaccurate.

The general argument in favour of a right to stop vehicles is put with particular clarity by Chris Ralph, policy adviser to the Society of Civil and Public Servants, in a Fabian pamphlet, *The Picket and the Law*. He starts with the by now familiar proposition that 'the idea of individual freedom is a middle class concept which is often in conflict with the fact of working-class advancement through solidarity', and goes on:

130

'The law of course embodies the middle-class value of the freedom of individual effort, but this need not be so. The law should provide a framework which protects the great majority from the actions of a minority'. The assumption that 'the great majority' of British people favour changes in the law giving more power to those who favour 'collective action' is not supported by the evidence of common observation, opinion polls, or voting behaviour; even so Mr Ralph's argument explains a point of view that is sincerely held.

The police, Mr Ralph says, have a 'unique' right to interfere with the liberty of a citizen 'when this interference is undertaken for the benefit of the majority'. The same could be said, he continues, about pickets,

particularly as they would not be obstructing an innocent citizen, but someone who was seeking to undermine collective industrial action. There is a popular assumption that everyone should be free from interference, including the strike-breaker, despite the fact that the latter's actions are to the detriment of others . . .

Pickets are only interested in those who are seeking to leave the public highway and enter a certain piece of land which is privately owned. At this intersection of land, it is common to find the employer's police force in position, with the power to obstruct. If management can employ private police on the gates, in the interests of protecting their profits, by for example stopping pilferage, it should be possible to have the gate manned by those who are interested in protecting the standard of living of the employees, with similar powers . . .

If pickets had a statutory right to detain vehicles, two pickets would be able to do what it needed two hundred to do in the past. There would be no need for the kind of mass picketing which closed the Saltley coke depot . . .

It follows that the law should be reformed so that pickets have a right to stop vehicles, which are intending to cross a picket line, for a reasonable period of time, in order that the pickets can communicate with the occupants of the vehicle.

The objection in principle to this line of argument is that it is contrary to the idea of democracy as the expression of the will of a majority of the people, with protection for minorities. The people elect their representatives. A majority of these pass a law giving the police, who are accountable at the end of the day to Parliament, a right to stop people in the streets, or move them on. Provided that the police act with the impartiality that such a law would demand, democracy remains in fair working order. If Parliament were to give such powers to interest groups, like official pickets, or trade unions, or employers' associations, or clubs formed by citizens who swore that they were motivated only by a desire to help, there could be no hope of impartiality and no protection for the weak.

It might be said that trade unions are not special interest groups, but, taking the TUC as a whole, representatives of roughly half the working population. This begs a number of questions about the representativeness of union officials, not to mention the rights of people who have no direct connection with the TUC at all. Even so, it might be argued, if Parliament chooses to give such powers to the TUC, surely that would be democratic? Since Britain has no written constitution or Bill of Rights the reply to this can only be that the spirit of the constitution would surely be breached by giving a power to a particular group of citizens to stop others in however good a cause.

Principle apart, there is the practical difficulty that the police would strongly oppose giving any power to pickets, or trade unions, or any others but themselves to stop vehicles. They also oppose taking such powers themselves, since this, they say, would entangle them in industrial disputes.

Shortly after returning to office in 1974 the Labour Cabinet debated the possibility of giving pickets the right to detain vehicles. The then Employment Secretary, Mr Michael Foot, was in favour; he was at that time acceding to most of the wishes of the TUC as part of the new Government's effort to maintain the political agreement between the unions and the Labour Party then known as the 'social contract'.

Sir Robert Mark, who was Commissioner of Police at the time, objected strongly. On 4 April 1974 he told a meeting of the Association of Chief Police Officers for England and Wales that he personally was prepared to take the unusual step of coming out in public against Mr Foot's proposals, no matter what the consequences. The other chief constables present supported this line.

They agreed that their President, then James Haughton of Merseyside, should write to the permanent under-secretary at the Home Office, explaining the police opposition. On 10 April he did so. Further letters followed, including one dated 26 June 1974, in which Sir Robert himself warned the Home Office that he would 'go public' if the new proposal became law, and another from James Haughton dated 27 June. On 10 March 1975 the police chiefs were called to the Home Office, where they explained their objections to the civil servants present. Mr Roy Jenkins, then Home Secretary, supported the police view that a right to stop vehicles interfered with the liberty of the individual, since he or she might not wish to be stopped. To the outraged police, the proposal required them to 'take orders from pickets'. In any event, it was asked, how would a distinction be made between pickets genuinely in dispute, and politically motivated pickets who came from elsewhere?

Following further exchanges between the Home Office and the Department of Employment, and their Ministers, the compromise clause that was eventually put forward, as part of the Employment Protection Bill, allowed pickets to 'seek by peaceful means, falling short of obstruction of the highway, to persuade any other person (whether in a vehicle or not) to stop for the purpose of peacefully obtaining or communicating information . . .' This was regarded as meaningless by those who wanted a guaranteed right to stop vehicles, so left-wing Labour MPs tried to strengthen the clause in committee. They failed, and in the end the Conservatives deleted it. Thus the police and Home Office view prevailed. To overcome opposition of this kind, a Labour Government would require an overall majority in the Commons, at a time when the civil libertarians in its own ranks were willing to accept such a change in the unwritten constitution.

A more likely settlement might be the development of an understood code of practice, possibly by arrangement between the police and the TUC, which already has its own internal code. This would start with the simple fact that in practice local constables often ask drivers if they will listen to pickets for a few minutes. Building on that, it might include an understanding about the maximum reasonable numbers, and the use of identifying armbands.

Such a concordat would be preferred by the TUC, which is traditionally chary of the extension of the law into territory it regards as its own, such as picketing. It might make some everyday squabbles easier to compress into civilized negotiations between police and pickets, or local trade union leaders. But without a general improvement in industrial law it would not prevent the use of mass demonstrations.

Until the law itself is made more sensitive demonstrations will no doubt recur. For the people likely to call them out believe that they are effective. For example, Mr Tom Durkin, chairman of the Brent Trades Council, told the Court of Inquiry on 18 July that ten months of picketing had been ignored. 'It is only since the extended and mass pickets have taken place that there is now a much greater interest and a determination to bring about a solution to this dispute. I would illustrate that by saying that I think even the High Court action was brought forward for two weeks and this inquiry itself I think is as a consequence of the extended and mass picketing.'

On the far left this kind of suspicion leads to flights of fantasy like the one in the *Socialist Worker* of 16 July, which read as follows

Is this coincidence?
11 July: The largest picket since the miners' blockade of Saltley 1972.
12 July: Lord Widgery rules in the High Court that the government advisory service ACAS did not act illegally in recommending that Grunwick recognize the union.

In short, two questions about the use of pickets emerge from the Grunwick affair.

The first is, would a new agreement between the police and the TUC be a useful means of lowering the temperature on most small picket lines? – to which a possible answer is 'perhaps'; tightening the law itself is better.

134

The second, more important, question, is based upon the necessary distinction between the undoubted right of people to assemble and protest, and the not so certain right, in a democracy in which unsatisfactory laws can eventually be improved through Parliament, to use the force of mass pickets in order to ensure victory in industrial disputes. The question is, at what stage should democratically elected Governments dig in their heels and say, 'No, we will not be influenced by such tactics?'

11 The argument – defects in the law

The liberal response might be to say that where laws are manifestly inadequate or unjust, and Parliament is slow to act, the only option left is some form of public protest. If that protest takes place, then a wise Government will recognize the cause, consider whether there is in fact a defect in the law, and put forward changes for Parliament's early approval. The irony of the Grunwick dispute is that where the law failed to bring justice, or where it seemed slow to do so, the fault could be traced to the trade union movement's deep reluctance to accept any legislation that might result in bringing industrial disputes before the courts. We can see this by looking at the two main claims made by the strikers, and in essence conceded by Lord Justice Scarman's Court of Inquiry: the claim for reinstatement of the employees who had been dismissed, and the claim for union recognition. In a third area, the legislation allowing the closed shop, the law has been changed to suit trade union demands, in a direction that has made many people suspicious of trade union motives.

The point, which is central to the argument about trade unions and the law, can be established by considering in turn each of these three areas.

Reinstatement

If you are dismissed it is usually possible to put in a claim to be given your job back, under the laws of unfair dismissal. The labour legislation of the 1970s, from the Conservatives' Industrial Relations Act through to the Labour Government's Trade Union and Labour Relations Act, the Employment Protection Act and the laws prohibiting discrimination on grounds of race or sex has such a powerful force that many small businessmen, unaware of the intricacies of the legislation, may possibly be forgiven for saying to themselves 'I am not going to take on any more people, because it is impossible to get rid of anyone nowadays.'

Such a view is of course an exaggeration. The truth is that the best practice of the most enlightened companies has been turned into law, so that arbitrary sackings are now very difficult to sustain, and the cost of compensation can be high. The law lays down the proper period of notice to be given. It tells employers that they must produce written reasons for dismissal, if asked, to any employee who has been with the company for half a year or more. There is an intricate web of rules on 'fair' and 'unfair' dismissal. Special industrial tribunals pass judgement on whether these rules have been broken. Employers may have to prove that the dismissal was on grounds the law considers fair, which might be incapacity to do the job, serious misconduct, redundancy (for which there is a separate mechanism for compensation and claims), or some other very good reason that might satisfy a tribunal. In the absence of such proof, or if the manner of the dismissal is considered to have been improper, a tribunal might award compensation against an employer. In the most extreme circumstances these could amount to a total of £12,000, though under £200 is most likely. Nor is this law just a matter of words on paper. Between autumn 1972 and autumn 1974 about 200 cases a week came up for conciliation between aggrieved individuals and companies. Then the new Trade Union and Labour Relations Act extended the right of complaint. Previously only those who had been with an employer for two years or more could claim unfair dismissal. Now the qualifying period was reduced to one year. Soon the number of cases referred to conciliation by the Advisory, Conciliation and Arbitration Service doubled, to around 400 a week. Then, in March 1975, the qualifying period was reduced to six months. The weekly rate of cases rose to about 700, a figure that increased again in 1976.

One of the few loopholes in this law allows employers to sack the whole of a group of workers who are on strike, or who have been locked out, or who are taking part in other 'industrial action'. This loophole is created by the Trade Union and Labour Relations Act 1974, as amended by the Employment Protection Act 1975. If there is an 'industrial action' in progress, the law lays down, an industrial tribunal shall not determine whether the sackings were fair or unfair unless it can be shown that there has been discrimination between employees – i.e. that some have been sacked and some not, or that some have been taken back and some not.

It was this provision of the law that led the Grunwick management to decide, after taking legal advice early on in the dispute, that it would sack all who were on strike, without exception. The position was maintained by Mr Ward during the whole of the troublesome year that followed; his argument was that if he went so far as to reinstate even one of the dismissed workers he would be taken before an industrial tribunal where he would be obliged to defend the sacking of all the others.

This fear was proved to be well founded by the application of fifty-nine of those on strike to an industrial tribunal on 23 March 1977 (an application whose particulars show the ample room for confusion in some aspects of the Grunwick case, since so many of the names seemed so very like each other). The attempt to win reinstatement through a tribunal was made because it was thought that Grunwick had in fact reinstated one employee, a Mr Dinesch Jam Solanki. It was said that he had stood with some of his friends on the picket line on 24 August, that he had joined APEX (membership card No. 590), and that in September he had collected £24, or two weeks' strike pay. After hearing the arguments of both sides, including Mr Solanki's categorical denial that he had received a membership card, or any strike pay, the tribunal decided that there had probably been a mix-up: a Mr Dilipkumar Solanki, a student who had joined the strike but subsequently disappeared, was probably the person who had received the membership card and the strike pay. Mr Dinesch Jam Solanki clearly did not want to join the strike. The tribunal found that there had been no discrimination in favour of any particular employee. Therefore, it had no jurisdiction in the claim of unfair dismissal. The fifty-nine lost their case.

The really important point about this loophole in the law is that *it is there because the trade unions want it to be there*. The idea was to keep the law out of industrial disputes, a notion that was accepted in the Tories' 1971 Act and repeated during the passage of the 1974 Act, as well as throughout most of 1975. If a tribunal had to decide whether a sacking of people who were on strike or locked out or engaged in an official go-slow was fair, then that same tribunal might have to pass judgement on the merits of the dispute. This at any rate was the original fear. Then it was realized that if such a provision was written into the new law, employers could sack people during strikes for reasons that had nothing to do with the immediate 'industrial action'. Thus the provision was made that all those who were dismissed had to be treated alike: you could not sack some people who were on strike but not others.

If that is, as it were, trade-union-made law, then it appears that companies are expected by the new Establishment to take it in a spirit favourable to trade unions. The Scarman report says of Grunwick:

By dismissing all those who went on strike they have excluded judicial review of the dismissals, but in our view they acted unreasonably in so doing. The dismissal of strikers, particularly within days of a strike starting, is extremely rare in practice, and by their own admission in evidence, they would have been willing to take some of the strikers back but refused to so do since, if they did, they would have to face proceedings by the others in an industrial tribunal in which the company would have to show in each case that the dismissal was fair. We ask – why not? Was it really unfair or unreasonable that a dismissed employee should have his individual case considered by a court or tribunal on its merits? Upon our analysis of the underlying causes of the strike the answer must be No.

This is a curious line of argument to come from a report signed by so distinguished a judge. For what it seems to say is that although the letter of the law is defective, companies are obliged to act according to the general notion of what is good

139

industrial practice, or pay the penalty of being labelled unreasonable. In earlier chapters it has been argued that the cause taken up by APEX was a just one: the strikers needed help, and it was morally right to help them. This is also the view expressed in the Scarman report. But from the very first days of the walkout, Mr Len Gristey, cognisant of the law as he was, warned that it might not be possible to get reinstatement for those who had been sacked for going on strike. We can now see that if the law is unhelpful on this point the reason is to be found in the attitude of the trade union movement to the law. As shall be shown later, there is an apparent difference between the Lord Justice Scarman who has argued eloquently about a Bill of Rights and the need to bring industrial relations within the law, and the Scarman report on Grunwick, which on the matter of unfair dismissals appears to say, 'if the law is defective, pay heed to the established view on industrial relations policy'.

Recognition

The right to join a trade union is universally recognized. It was disputed by no one in the Grunwick case, not even the company itself. An allied right, which is to have a union recognized by a company as an agent for collective bargaining on behalf of its members is also widely established, although if Grunwick accepted this, then its behaviour after APEX asked for recognition suggests that at best it did so with reluctance. Yet these rights are to be found in the loftiest of documents. The freedom of association is written into the Universal Declaration of Human Rights, drawn up under the authority of the United Nations. The right to form and join trade unions is derived from this freedom. The same right, as well as the right of collective bargaining can be found in the laws or constitutions of countries such as West Germany, France, Italy, Sweden and the United States.

Britain has ratified a number of international conventions guaranteeing such rights, including the European Social Charter and the Council of Europe's Convention for the Protection of Human Rights and Fundamental Freedoms, as well as two

International Labour Conventions, Nos. 87 and 98, which cover the freedom of association and the right to organize and bargain collectively. For example, the relevant article of International Labour Convention No. 98 reads:

Article 1

1. Workers shall enjoy adequate protection against acts of anti-union discrimination in respect of their employment.

2. Such protection shall apply more particularly in respect of acts calculated to

(a) make the employment of a worker subject to the condition that he shall not join a union or shall relinquish trade union membership;

(b) cause the dismissal of or otherwise prejudice a worker by reason of union membership or because of participation in union activities outside working hours or, with the consent of the employer, within working hours.

It is arguable that for most of this century the policy of successive British governments has been to acquiesce in, and at times even encourage, the development of collective bargaining, at least in public authorities (through the Whitley Council system), and in some large-scale industries. When it repealed the Combination Laws in 1824 Britain became probably the first European country to remove the barrier to the legal formation of trade unions. The recent legal extension of trade union freedoms was alluded to in Chapter 9; the distinctive feature of British experience that is relevant to the present argument is that for most of our modern industrial history trade union independence has been brought about by carving areas of immunity away from the common law. It was not so much a question of saying 'you have a right to form a union or to go on strike' as, rather, saying 'if you do those things you will not be taken to court for doing them'. This legal tradition is the principal reason why to this day British trade unions prefer to separate their activities from the law, and to exist in a constitutional world of their own.

Thus trade union rights have been established in Britain either in defiance of the law, as in the early part of the nineteenth century, or after an understanding or legal process whose

141

effect was that the law would not interfere. In many other countries, particularly on the continent of Europe and in the United States, the law stepped in after public pressure or in response to public opinion and stated specifically that trade unions had a role within the legal system or the constitution. In Britain the trade unions managed on their own. It is of some interest for students of the Grunwick dispute that this extra-legal advance of trade unions has come about in three broad phases, with the skilled workers leading the way in the nineteenth century. The unskilled manual workers followed at the turn of the century. The white-collar workers and workers in small companies are now being invited by the unions to come to the industrial battle-front. The sense of history that is characteristic of most union leaders tells them that all that has been achieved in the past has come about in spite of the law rather than because of it and that therefore this is the way matters can develop from now on, in spite of the recent introduction of laws that positively favour trade unionism.

So the first successful attempt to establish rights of recognition by statute, the Conservatives' Industrial Relations Act of 1971, was rejected by the trade union movement, partly because it saw little need for the assistance of the law and partly because that Act not only gave rights to unions, but also imposed restraints and obligations on them.

Yet the Act was a turning point in British legal history. It stated the right to belong to a trade union, and, following American practice under Roosevelt's National Labour Relations Act 1935, it provided for recognition of unions by unwilling employers. Much of the spirit of this legislation had been proposed by the previous Labour Government, following the Donovan Report, but because the trade unions would not have it the first action of the Labour Government that returned to power in 1974 was the repeal of the Industrial Relations Act. It was a selective repeal, however: by and large the clauses giving rights to employees and legal immunities to the trade unions were retained, while those imposing responsibilities and restraints were discarded.

Such was the atmosphere in which the Advisory, Conciliation

and Arbitration Service was conceived. ACAS took over the long-established conciliation and advisory services of the Department of Employment, and some of the functions of the former Commission of Industrial Relations. It regards itself as independent, since its governing council is comprised of three trade union leaders nominated by the Confederation of British Industry, and three academics. The latter are presumably not appointed in the belief that they have a cast of mind that is inexorably opposed to the policies of the Government of the day.

This is not the only reason why the service's 'independence' is notional. The staff of ACAS have the status of civil servants. The Governing Council is the quintessence of 'corporatism' – that notion of a state in which government by representatives of industry with like-minded academics thrown in as makeweights, supersedes government by the directly elected representatives of the citizens. And when it comes to trade union recognition, the service does not pretend to be neutral: in its 1976 annual report a chapter on the subject reminds the reader of Section 1 of the Employment Protection Act 1975, which gives ACAS the general duty of 'promoting the improvement of industrial relations, and in particular of encouraging the extension of collective bargaining and the development and, where necessary, the reform of collective bargaining machinery'.

It would be wrong to give the impression that the *only* function of ACAS is to promote collective bargaining. It is a far more complicated body than that, with wide responsibilities in every area of industrial relations. In its day-to-day handling of business it is probably as fair-minded as any other official or quasi-official body. But its role in recognition disputes is the matter at issue in the Grunwick affair, and it is on this part of its work alone that we must focus here.

Because of its origins ACAS will naturally approach any application for trade union recognition in the hope that at the end of the day the affected company will agree that collective bargaining by trade unions is the best method of conducting relations between employers and employees: this is, after all, part of the reason for its existence. The trade union movement had

143

some hopes when ACAS was being given statutory backing in 1975 that such a body would help promote the unionization of the many small companies in Britain, since it is here that one of the largest harvests is to be reaped.

So far, so straightforward. The difficulty is that there was a general reluctance to give ACAS powers to enforce the recognition that the unions so badly wanted. If you give powers you must have penalties; the result could be that recalcitrant employers might be fined, or at the worst extreme, imprisoned. For once, *employers* could become martyrs. And if you do that to employers you may open a Pandora's box; there might be a general outcry in favour of similar legal constraints over the activities of trade unions. Given Britain's industrial relations history and the passionately anti-legal mood of the trade unions in the aftermath of the repeal of the Industrial Relations Act there was little inclination in 1974 and 1975 to grant ACAS powers of enforcement over either side of industry.

The result was another flawed piece of legislation. ACAS was designed to work by means of conciliation, mediation, discussion, reasonable argument. If all else failed it could make a unilateral recommendation that an employer must accept a certain union as the bargaining agent for that company's employees, but there is little clarity about what would happen if such a recommendation was ignored. In theory the Employment Protection Act contains the threat that a higher body known as the Central Arbitration Committee can lay down terms and conditions for the employment of the people who have been denied union recognition, but in August 1977 the efficacy of this law had yet to be tested. Yet this did not mean the service was without another kind of power; the power of established opinion.

As to its method of working, ACAS was left more or less to itself. This meant that it had to spend its early years building up its own case-law, partly by means of internal argument, and partly as a result of court actions against it. The British predeliction for not making clear rules about anything, magnified by the trade union predilection for keeping clear of the rules altogether, almost guaranteed challenges to ACAS on the manner in which it was exercising its responsibilities.

144

The principal challenge came from Grunwick. It might be argued that it was not a wholly disinterested challenge – that the company was fighting off what it saw as the unwarranted intrusion of a trade union into its affairs rather than testing the legality and fairness of the methods adopted by ACAS – but that hardly alters the case. If the law had been framed in a more logical manner, saying flatly as the laws of so many other countries do that it is illegal to deny union recognition in such and such circumstances; or if the law had laid down that ACAS has power to demand cooperation from employers in its inquiries; or if the principles upon which ACAS must determine its recommendations had been codified, none of the arguments between the company and the service could have taken place. In this sense it can be said that the whole of the protracted battle over recognition of APEX could have been prevented if only the law was precise (although in the US, where the law *is* clear, there are many legal battles).

Because it is not precise, the misunderstanding, delay, and what the Scarman report, begging a hundred questions, called 'a failure to respond to the spirit of the law' was almost inevitable. If you take a spirited organization like ACAS, infused with the idea that collective bargaining is a sacred duty of businessmen, and send it into the jungle of small businesses armed with the broad barrelled clauses of the Employment Protection Act and the more deadly weapon of established opinion, it is inevitable that it will soon run into a scrap with a tiger.

The tiger did not always fight in a gentlemanly manner, but then that is not in the nature of the beast. The company's dispute with ACAS by telephone and letter, always questioning the likely fairness of any investigation by a body whose purpose seemed to be to accord trade union rights wherever possible, was dragged on until very near Christmas 1976, after which ACAS decided to go ahead on its own. Its subsequent report, published in March, recommended recognition of APEX, and Grunwick then asked the High Court for a declaration that the recommendation was null and void.

As summarized by the Lord Chief Justice, Lord Widgery, on 12 July 1977, there were three grounds on which the company had based its case. The first was to do with the form of the questions and the posting of the questionnaire that ACAS had sent out; Grunwick called expert evidence from polling organizations to indicate that the methods used would have a leading effect and incline people towards an affirmative answer; a postal questionnaire also made it more practical for interested parties to intimidate those who filled in the forms. Lord Widgery found that ACAS was given such wide discretion over the methods it chose to ascertain the opinions of the people it canvassed that the courts could not question its conclusions unless it had 'misdirected itself', which he said it had not.

Lord Widgery was bound to accept the English tradition which relies on the integrity and goodwill of the people who have been put in charge. This is different from the continental or American tradition, which would be to lay down written rules of conduct for a ballot of workers' opinion and expect the administrators to stick by them.

The second issue, said the Lord Chief Justice, was whether the members of APEX, most of whom had been dismissed and were on strike, could reasonably be asked their opinion by ACAS. Grunwick had always maintained that since these employees had been sacked – and sacked well before the application by APEX for a recommendation on recognition from ACAS – they were no longer relevant to the case. In fact these were the only people ACAS canvassed, and they came out 93–0 in favour of APEX. Lord Widgery said that he had no doubt that the men and women in question were what the Employment Protection Act calls 'workers to whom the issue relates' since they wanted to return to work at Grunwick.

As for the third issue, the question was whether ACAS's failure to obtain the opinion of the workers who had not gone on strike but were still in Grunwick's employ nullified its report. Mr Ward had declined to give the names and addresses of these employees. In Court his Counsel had referred to that list as the last card in his hand. If that was a true analogy, said Lord Widgery, Mr Ward might have done himself great harm by refusing to play that card. If he had handed over the list of workers in December ACAS would have made an attempt to discover the opinion of the two thirds of the Grunwick employees who had stayed at work. It was at least possible that the result would have favoured Mr Ward, 'perhaps heavily'. Grunwick's application was dismissed.

What would ACAS have done if it had received that list and then conducted a ballot of the willing workers as well as those on strike, with the result that two thirds said 'no' to APEX and one third said 'yes'? The possibility is that it would have recommended recognition anyway. By August 1977 the service had received about 850 applications from trade unions, and reported on sixty of them. All but a dozen of those reports were in the unions' favour. One important application for recognition that failed was at IBM UK Ltd, where ASTMS and other unions were hoping for new recruits. According to the ACAS report of July 1977, 13,734 IBM employees were sent questionnaires, with a response rate of around 95 per cent. At Greenock, the voting against having a union in the company was 90·2 per cent; in the rest of the company it was 95·9 per cent. ACAS could hardly recommend recognition at IBM. (About a third of the cases it resolves result in 'no recommendation'; nearly 300 claims have been resolved, mostly informally.)

Yet, true to the tradition of clarifying as few rules as possible, there is no known figure below which ACAS will not recommend a union's acceptance, and no known figure above which it will ask a company to recognize the applicant. In the United States it is simple: if a majority of the employees vote 'yes' under the National Labour Relations Act procedures there will be a union; if 'no', no. ACAS will, as the British tradition has it, weigh all the relevant facts and consider the circumstances as it sees fit. This means that if it thinks that a union has a chance of taking root it could recommend in favour, even if the 'yes' vote is one third or less.

There is no clear guideline about whether such a recommendation would mean that the union would then bargain on behalf of all the workers in the company or only on behalf of its members. Trade unions approve of this lack of clarity because companies are hardly likely to pay non-members less than members (since if they did the non-members would join up), while if they pay the same amount the union can add recruits every time it wins a wage increase or some other benefit by saying: our efforts have won you this advantage; surely in all conscience you should join us?

It is also reasonable to say of ACAS that its predilection will be in favour of a trade union that it regards as independent, partly because of the terms of the law and partly because in the world in which it operates the idea of a 'company union' is anathema. (Such a union is illegal in the United States, under the National Labour Relations Act.) Thus even if the works council at Grunwick had functioned effectively a demand for a union by what ACAS chose to regard as a reasonable fraction of its employees would probably have resulted in a recommendation that the union be recognized. Only if the management so satisfied the workers that they overwhelmingly rejected a union, as in the IBM case, would there be any guarantee of avoiding such a recommendation. But the sophisticated personnel policies of IBM, with their emphasis on close employee–manager relations and an easily understood mechanism for sending grievances right to the top, is not available for small businesses like Grunwick. IBM offers a career; small companies might have a high turnover of staff. (In 1976 ACAS was receiving recognition claims at an average rate of forty a month, mostly affecting small and medium-sized businesses – IBM was one of the exceptions – and more than half of them involved white-collar workers.)

None of this calmed the tiger down. Following its setback in the High Court Grunwick went to the Appeal Court, where it fared rather better. The judgement of 20 July 1977 deserves inspection. Lord Denning, the Master of the Rolls, seemed uncertain about Grunwick's claim, unsuccessfully put forward in the High Court, that ACAS should not have canvassed the opinion of those on strike because they were not 'workers to whom the issue relates'. His two fellow-judges, Lord Justice Browne and Lord Justice Geoffrey Lane, were in no doubt. Both agreed that dismissed workers seeking re-employment were in law and in common sense 'workers to whom the issue relates'. This afforded much relief to ACAS, which on the basis of the judgement could in future canvass the opinions of sacked workers or workers on strike if there was a recognition claim. But the judgement as a whole went against the service, on the ground that the opinions of the workers who remained at their posts had not been ascertained. The contest had been seen by too many people as one between two parties only, said Lord Denning. But there was a 'silent third party' – the workers inside the factory. They too were entitled to have their views considered. The Appeal Court did not think that the fact that it was Mr Ward himself who had denied ACAS the names and addresses of his workers made any difference.

Here again we return to the disadvantage of acting without written rules that everyone can understand and accept. Britain is probably the only country in the world that could devise something like ACAS and deny it the legal right to demand the information on which to base its operations. The Appeal Court judgement was taken to the House of Lords, but whatever the decision there (this is being written before the case is heard) the point remains the same. If the simple rule that companies must cooperate in a ballot of their workers had been written into the Employment Protection Act Grunwick would not have been able to withhold the names and addresses, and the argument, which lasted for more than a year, would not have been possible. The trouble is that in fairness you cannot have a simple rule like that on its own. Putting in one rule means putting in others; that is why during the early years of the 'Social Contract' the TUC managed to convince the Labour Government (if it needed convincing) that it was better to have no such rules at all.

The closed shop

One of the aspects of the early stages of the propaganda war between APEX and Grunwick that most irritated the trade union side was the implication that APEX was seeking a closed shop in the company. It was not; it was asking for no more than recognition as the bargaining agent for its members at Grunwick, although it naturally had hopes of attracting more members once it had its foot in the door. But Brent Trades Council and strike committee members as well as APEX officials all along realized that there was what they regarded as a 'hard core of anti-union employees' inside Grunwick, people who they would be unlikely to recruit. And after the Scarman report appeared at the end of August 1977 Mr Grantham himself said that if the company accepted the union and the phased re-employment of its members APEX would not seek a closed shop. Yet the trade union movement as a whole favours the closed shop. It was made legal again by the Labour Government after it had been curtailed under the Industrial Relations Act. And APEX has sought it in companies other than Grunwick.

The closed shop is a distinctly Anglo-American method of limiting the freedom of the individual worker. In practice it is difficult to find employment in certain companies or industries on the West European continent without belonging to a union, but the idea that someone can be deprived of his livelihood if he or she declines to join a particular trade union is anathema over there. This writer recalls the leader of the most left-wing of the Dutch trade union confederations saying 'Dutchmen won't stand for such coercion.' In France, where unions are divided along political lines, the closed shop is not practical. In West Germany the right to stay out of a trade union is written into the constitution (as is the right to join). The Universal Declaration of Human Rights includes the freedom to refuse to join an association.

Britain's adherence to this anti-democratic device has in recent years taken an especially unpleasant form, particularly under provisions such as the one in the Employment Protection Act that make it impossible to sue an employer for unfair dismissal if you are sacked for not belonging to a union with which that employer has a closed-shop agreement. This has in practice meant some long-standing but independent-minded workers being dismissed (by British Railways, for example) for their unwillingness to join a specified union.

Learned specialists on the closed shop write lengthy treatises saying that it makes for good industrial relations, because the trade union officials and the employer can manage the lives of the workers between them, without interference. Trade unionists who defend it (not all of them do) say either that they need the device to win bargaining strength, or that if some people stay out of a union that wins advantages for most workers they become unpopular 'free riders' whose presence in the company can be a 'provocation'. The first point can be answered by indicating that bargaining strength comes from employee feeling; even if everyone belongs to a union there cannot be a successful strike if the workers do not want it, as a refusal to strike in the face of shop stewards' demands at the Longbridge plant of British Leyland in August 1977 showed. As for 'free riders', there are several ways out, like a deduction from wages of an amount equivalent to union subscriptions.

The existence of a compulsory institution like the closed shop is one reason why the trade union movement's claim that it is truly democratic in spirit is not easy to accept. The Grunwick workers who do not want a union are people with rights just like those who do. If they fear the future intentions of APEX (whatever Mr Grantham might say), this is not hard to understand, given the general approach of the trade union movement to the closed shop.

Once again, the attitude of our trade union movement to the law has resulted in a state of affairs that is not really in the interests of modern trade unionism. If we had a set of rules for the conduct of trade union affairs, and a rule making the work of bodies like ACAS much more straightforward, plus a legal recognition of the right not to join or to join a union industrial relations would be more equitable. This argument will be examined further in Chapter 13. Meanwhile, we must consider the blacking of Grunwick's mail, a case in which once again the rule of law was judged by the Government and the trade union movement to be of lesser importance than the need to avoid doing anything that might upset too many trade union members.

12   The argument – the postal blacking

On at least one of the issues arising out of the Grunwick dispute the law is quite clear. The refusal to handle the company's mail was illegal during the four-day blacking in November 1976 and again during the seven-week blacking in June and July 1977. It is also clear that the Government declined to take the postmen to court over this breach of the law. What is not quite so clear is whether the Government was justified in standing back.

Throughout the blacking by the postmen in midsummer 1977, an action that caused inconvenience to many innocent residents of north London and strain to businesses in the area, the official attitude was 'above all do not go to court. Do nothing that will stir them up.' And so in spite of headline scares about a national postal strike the dispute was kept local. No postal worker was taken to court. The Attorney-General did not intervene. The Post Office was even refused the right to relinquish its statutory monopoly over the mail so that others could do the work it was prevented from doing.

It did lock out the workers who had refused to handle Grunwick mail. They were paid by the union, which consistently told the men that their action was illegal and as consistently told Ministers that there was little that could be done about it. In the end, after some ugly scenes between local branch leaders and national officials, the blacking was called off, without benefit of the assistance of the law. The mollifying methods of the new Establishment had been allowed to work.

To return to the law: Section 58 of the Post Office Act of 1953 reads:

If any officer of the Post Office, contrary to his duty, opens, or procures or suffers to be opened, any postal packet in course of transmission by post, or wilfully detains or delays or procures or suffers to be detained or delayed, any such postal packet, he shall be guilty of a misdemeanour and be liable to imprisonment, or to a fine, or to both.

It is also against the law to talk someone into holding up the mail. Section 68 of the Act says:

If any person solicits or endeavours to procure any other person to commit an offence punishable on indictment under this Act, he shall be guilty of a misdemeanour and be liable to imprisonment for a term not exceeding two years.

Nor can you do it with telegrams; Section 45 of the Telegraph Act, 1863, makes it an offence for any person in the employment of the Post Office wilfully or negligently to omit or delay to transmit or deliver any message or prevent or delay the transmission or delivery of any message.

When the Union of Post Office Workers officially supported the blacking of Grunwick's mail in November 1976 the Government did nothing. There was no official prosecution. The Attorney-General did not intervene. So Grunwick, backed by the National Association for Freedom, issued a writ against the union. Previously the idea that it could be against the law for postmen to behave in this way seems not to have entered the head of the General Secretary of the UPW, and it apparently was not in the minds of senior officials at the Department of Employment. But as soon as the writ was issued, and the lawyers pointed their index fingers at Sections 58 and 68, things began to move. Taking as a cover for their retreat an indication that Grunwick would henceforth cooperate with ACAS (an indication apparently received from ACAS itself) the UPW called on its members to return to normal work, and the case eventually fell away.

A more celebrated action took place the following January. Mr John Gouriet, of the NAFF, discovered on 13 January that the UPW executive had resolved to call on its members not to handle mail to South Africa during the week beginning Sunday 16 January. This was in response to a TUC call for support for an international trade union plan to hold a week of

153

'action' in protest against the repression of trade unionists by the South African Government. (There is a great deal to be said in favour of such a week of protest, and in this writer's view the pity is that the international trade union movement has not yet found the unity, or the disinterested spirit, necessary to act even more strongly against the apartheid policies of the South African government.)

On the afternoon of Friday 14 January, Mr John Gouriet applied to the Attorney-General, Mr Sam Silkin, for his leave to bring what the lawyers call 'relator proceedings' – an action in which the Attorney-General's name appears at the top of the paper, as representing the public interest, but also one over which the 'relator', i.e. Mr Gouriet, would do the actual suing, assisted by his own lawyers. Mr Silkin denied his consent to Mr Gouriet. He later explained to Parliament that one of his reasons for so doing was that the Post Office had intended to put up notices warning its workers that to obey the union instructions would be a criminal offence. 'And as the week of action was not due to start until midnight on the Sunday following,' Mr Silkin said in the Commons on 27 January, 'it was not and could not yet be known whether Post Office workers would heed their employer's warning . . .' Anyway, if on the Monday morning, the Post Office thought that offences were being committed, it would have various ways of taking the relevant employees to court, for some of which Mr Silkin's consent would not be needed.

'On the face of information available to me, and in my judgement, the taking of injunction proceedings in my name had the inherent risk, at that early stage, of inflaming the situation before the need for it was demonstrated and might well result in breaches of the law and inconvenience to the public over a much wider area than the two sections of Post Office employees affected . . .' said Mr Silkin.

None of this was told to Mr Gouriet at the time, and if it had been Mr Gouriet might not have accepted the reasoning as sound. The prerogative of the Attorney-General is to make such decisions without explaining himself to any person or court, reserving anything he might choose to say for Parliament if his decisions are contested there. Clearly the NAFF did not accept this, for Mr Gouriet went ahead and issued a writ under his own name against the UPW. The application was turned down that very afternoon by Mr Justice Stocker, to no one's surprise since most people in the legal profession believe that only a public authority, the Attorney-General, can bring cases affecting public rights, in this case the right to the use of the mail and telecommunications services.

Mr Gouriet was not deterred. Acting with a persistence that was perhaps reinforced by the memory of Ross McWhirter, he went to the Appeal Court. On Saturday morning, the Master of the Rolls, Lord Denning, sitting with Lord Justice Lawton and Lord Justice Ormrod, granted a temporary injunction. The boycott was called off. 'Is the Attorney-General to be the final arbiter as to whether the law should be enforced or not?' asked Lord Denning. Yes, answered the Attorney-General the following week, when he came to argue before Lord Denning and his two colleagues. In matters like this he was answerable to Parliament, and not the courts. Mr Silkin was right, but for a while there was doubt about the matter, and a great deal of portentous debate on it, because the Court of Appeal, and in particular Lord Denning, took a contrary view. The idea that the Attorney-General was answerable to Parliament alone was, to his mind, a direct challenge to the rule of law, he said in his judgement given on 27 January. 'Let me take some instances,' he went on.

'Only hypothetically, of course, but to test this claim of his suppose that he refused his consent for corrupt motives or in bad faith. The Attorney-General went so far as to say that even this would not be questioned. That is an extreme hypothesis which can be put on one side. But take a lesser hypothesis. Suppose that he refused his consent for party-political reasons and not in the interests of the public at large. Is he then to be answerable to Parliament alone? Where he would, perchance, be supported by his own political party? Or, even a still lesser hypothesis: suppose he refused his consent because he considered that the information was laid by a pressure group, of which he disapproved: but yet it was a matter which ought to be taken up in the interests of the public at large. Would his refusal then be justifiable?

'In all these cases he would be failing in his duty, as I have earlier stated it. Does it mean then that nothing can be done about it? That no one can come to the courts and inform us of it? I should have thought that in order to dispel suspicion, he could come and tell us what his reasons were: or at least outline them without disclosing anything confidential or secret. But that he declines to do.

'These instances are, of course, entirely hypothetical. I would not suggest for one moment that they existed here . . .'

It was in this judgement that Lord Denning reminded the Attorney-General of the words of Thomas Fuller, 'Be you ever so high, the law is above you.' It was wishful thinking. In modern Britain the law is not above trade unions or their members or officers acting in trade disputes, or indeed sometimes in circumstances outside trade disputes. It has expressly been put to one side of the union movement, and where there has been an obvious oversight, as in the case of postal workers blacking Grunwick mail, no Labour Government is likely to respond to a breach with anything other than 'this is very serious. We must amend the law. Meanwhile would you mind very much considering perhaps the possibility of going to work and handling the company's mail if we ask you very nicely?' The Denning judgement, having questioned this approach, could not be allowed to stand. And in the House of Lords on 26 July it was duly overturned, with the remarks of Lord Wilberforce about Lord Denning equalling in their imperviousness the earlier remarks of Lord Denning about Mr Silkin. Never mind, the prerogative of the Attorney-General was safe. It was not even under challenge by the time the intricate case reached the Lords. As Lord Wilberforce pointed out, changes in the case meant that by that time there was no longer a claim that the Attorney-General's refusal to consent to relator proceedings was improper, or that it could be reviewed by the court.

That issue, originally presented as one of great constitutional importance, had disappeared from the case. The importance remained, but the issue had vanished, said Lord Wilberforce

156

acidly. The Attorney-General's decision was accepted as unassailable in the courts. All that Mr Gouriet was then claiming was that Mr Silkin's refusal to act did not bar Mr Gouriet himself from acting. This claim too was turned down.

And so another great British squabble died away. It had much exercised the minds of lawyers for the TUC, who worried about whether any private citizen could use Lord Denning's judgement as a means of winning back through the courts some of the control over trade union behaviour that had been signed away by Parliament, especially in the legislation of 1974–6. This fear, which led to much private whispering inside the new Establishment in the first half of 1977, was laid to rest by the Lords' judgement. But it was a false fear.

The reason why the main fear aroused by the long squabble was false is that there never was any serious doubt about the Attorney-General's prerogative. Sad to say, few people questioned whether that prerogative ought to continue in its present form, for that is the real problem. To appreciate it, one must start with an exposition of the rationale behind the prerogative as it exists today.

It runs as follows. In every society there must be an arrangement whereby someone can decide to bend the rules. For instance, if it is known that Parliament has made homosexual practices between consenting adults legal in Great Britain, but not in Northern Ireland, it may be wrong to prosecute for such offences in Northern Ireland, especially if the same law is about to be extended to that part of the kingdom. If Parliament indicates in April that by December there will be no more hangings, it may be right to commute all death sentences after April. Right from the village policemen looking the other way if a child steals an apple from a farmer's tree to, say, an Attorney-General declining to use Section 11 of the Official Secrets Act in circumstances in which it is known that the section is to be changed, the case for flexibility in the application of the law is consistent. To say, 'these are the rules. There is no way around them' is regarded as too rigid for modern societies. This is particularly so in industrial relations where a court might create martyrs. In the case of the postmen acting in sympathy with the

157

Grunwick strikers, there was a risk that a national postal strike might be provoked if they were taken to court and charged with a breach of Section 58 of the Post Office Act. Someone must decide whether such a risk is worth taking; in Britain this is regarded as essentially a political decision to be taken by the politically based Attorney-General.

Enlightened supporters of the rule of law will see the force of these arguments. At the end of the day, the law cannot be applied if it is not believed by most people to be just and reasonable. A law that prevents postmen from going on strike, or seems to do so may appear to be unfair. (Actually they are probably safe to walk out, although they break the law if they stay in the sorting room and decline to handle particular letters.) If the law is unfair, perhaps it should be amended? (The Labour Government has promised to oblige.) In America, the place where such delicate matters are settled is the Supreme Court, which certainly follows public opinion and the dictates of expediency, as its changing judge-made law on the death penalty has shown.

By bringing in the American Supreme Court the flaw in the British arrangement is at once made apparent. Appointments to that Court are made by the President and therefore political, but once on the Court an American justice is independent of all pressures, party or otherwise. This is perhaps one reason why the Supreme Court has made courageous decisions such as those leading to the desegregation of the schools. A British Attorney-General can never be that independent. He is a party politician. The Prime Minister appoints him and can dismiss him. He is answerable to Parliament, but then Parliament itself has in recent years become the captive of the party in office. The traditional respect for constitutional proprieties has waned. Our Attorney-Generals may be the most upstanding of men, and Mr Sam Silkin is no doubt the very model of integrity – but the point is that under present British arrangements the *opportunity for political corruption is always present.* By political corruption is meant keeping the friends of the party in power out of court, be those friends a company, a union, local government officials or a group of individuals.

In less intemperate times, when the rule of law was an overriding principle, to say 'that couldn't happen here' might have sufficed. Today, as the political conflict is soured by the class conflict, and as respect for earlier notions of political propriety is dwindling, it is not good enough. We may or may not trust the political conscience of this or that Attorney-General of the past; what cannot be guaranteed is the behaviour of Mr Silkin's successors, of either party. This is particularly true in the case of industrial and trade union activity, since the unions have strained so hard to place themselves outside the law. If that is where they wish to be, it is trebly important that people whose convenience or livelihoods might be affected by trade union action should have a greater safeguard than the judgement of a political Attorney-General. This is one of the several arguments in favour of bringing trade unions into the mainstream of law, arguments that will be followed more closely in the next, and final, chapter.

13 The resolution: a new constitutional settlement

The comment in the Scarman report on what it calls the 'legal aspect' of the Grunwick dispute provides a classic short text for any discussion of the place of trade unions within the law. The relevant paragraphs of the report are 55 to 58, and 64. They read:

55. In the field of industrial relations the law has to effect a reconciliation and adjustment of a number of fundamental human rights and basic freedoms. Inevitably the stance of the company has been associated with some of these rights and freedoms and the stance of the union with others.

56. The rights and freedoms with which the stance of the company has been associated are:

(1) the right to the peaceful enjoyment of property, which includes the right to conduct a legitimate business within the law as one judges best: see Article 1, 1st Protocol, European Convention on Human Rights;

(2) the freedom to refuse to join an association (which in its industrial application becomes the right not to join a union): see the Universal Declaration of Human Rights 1948, Article 20(2);

(3) the right to free choice of employment: see the Universal Declaration, 23(1).

57. Those with which the union stance has been associated are:

(1) the freedom of association, which in its industrial application becomes the right to join a union: see European Convention, Article 11, and the Universal Declaration, Articles 20(1) and 23(4);

(2) the freedom of peaceful assembly, one of the industrial applications of which is peaceable picketing: see European Convention, Article 11, and the Universal Declaration, Article 20(1) and

(3) the right to just and favourable conditions of work: see

Universal Declaration, Article 23(1) and the European Social Charter 1961.

58. The English reconciliation of these rights and freedoms has been traditionally sought through the development of voluntary collective bargaining but this process is now supported principally by two statutes, which themselves have to be interpreted in the context of the common law – the back-cloth of English law. The statutes are the Trade Union and Labour Relations Act 1974 and the Employment Protection Act 1975. The policy of the law is to exclude 'trade disputes' – or industrial disputes, as they are more familiarly known – from judicial review by the courts, while leaving to individual workers a recourse to the courts (i.e. industrial tribunals) to pursue certain individual grievances. There is substituted for judicial review of trade disputes an advisory, conciliation and arbitration process with ACAS as the statutory body to operate it. All rights and freedoms for which each side contends are recognized by English law, but failing agreement their adjustment to each other is to be sought by the processes of conciliation and arbitration under the guidance of ACAS. The sanctions of the law (such as they are) are indirect and are not those associated with the execution or enforcement of a judgement delivered by a court of law. An inevitable consequence of the system is that, where the process fails to secure agreement, industrial action is the one weapon left to resolve the dispute. Industrial action is a form of organized self-help – e.g. the lock-out, the strike, 'blacking' and the picket. And there is always a risk that self-help, if not coupled with self-restraint, may end in violence. English law, if it is to work, requires of parties to an industrial dispute a modicum of self-restraint in the pursuit of their rights. Men must act reasonably within the law. The British tradition of compromise is implicit in the modern English law governing industrial relations.

64. On the legal aspect of the dispute we conclude that both the company and the union have in certain respects failed to respond to the spirit of the law. By dismissing all the strikers on 2 September and refusing to negotiate the reinstatement of any of them, and by refusing to accept ACAS offers of conciliation, the company has contributed to the prolonging, deepening, and widening of the dispute with all its attendant risk of violence and disorder. By seeking in 1977 further UPW action in blacking Grunwick mail the union ignored the legal decision in the case of Gouriet v. UPW, and in calling for the mass picket it initiated action, the subsequent course of which has greatly disturbed the nation.

As a description of the best received opinion of the new Establishment these paragraphs can hardly be faulted even though it is a sobering comment on that opinion that a report signed by a distinguished jurist is obliged to aver that by adhering to the law Grunwick 'contributed to the prolonging, deepening, and widening of the dispute with all its attendant risk of violence and disorder'.

For what this really means is that it is necessary for citizens to ascertain what the general opinion on the spirit of the law happens to be at the time, and abide by that, rather than by what Parliament has enacted. The absolute letter of the law is often absurd, as Shylock discovered, but the degree to which people must be expected to set it aside in the interest of what so-and-so says is its spirit should be very limited. The alternative is rule by those with the greatest muscle.

This writer can find no better authority for saying as much than Lord Scarman: not the Lord Scarman who with two fellow-members of the Court of Inquiry signed the report on Grunwick, but the Sir Leslie Scarman who was so universally praised for his wisdom in delivering the Hamlyn Lectures, 'English Law – The New Dimension', just three years previously. Can it be the same man? Here is what he said in those lectures:

In a judge discretion is the better part of valour: I shall, therefore, say little about the repeal of the Industrial Relations Act 1971, and nothing about the legislation which has replaced it. But the chaos and confusion that has been endemic in industrial relations for many years are not to be disregarded in the context of my argument. Everyone agrees, I hope and believe, that an appropriate place has to be found for industrial relations within the law. The question not yet resolved is: where is that place to be? More specifically, we have not yet decided whether industrial relations are to be regulated in accordance with a law interpreted and applied within a unified legal system, or 'extra-legally', i.e. in accordance with some specialized system of control isolated from the general legal system. If we opt for the latter, there are, I suggest, two likely consequences. First, we shall be witnessing yet another move away from a general legal system to specialized and detached systems – a trend already to be detected in current attitudes to common market law, the social security system, and the regulation of land use. Secondly, there will arise a real risk of forces of great power in our society escaping from the rule of law altogether. Such consequences, if they ensue, would, there can be no doubt, constitute a weakening of the capacity of law to impose restraint on the exercise of power in society. The Industrial Relations Act 1971 was an attempt to subject the power of the trade unions to the rule of law as interpreted and applied by a court forming part of the general legal system of the land. The unions have overthrown it. It does not, however, follow that because this piece of legislation has proved to be unavailing and unacceptable the case for the rule of law in industrial relations is unsound. What is clear is that the general legal system conceived as one based on common law principles has not proved an acceptable instrument of control: but the need for control, and control according to law, will remain so long as men believe that uncontrolled power is an evil to be eradicated from civilized society. The challenge which faces lawyers is to win and retain public confidence in the law as the instrument of control. I say no more of industrial relations than that the failures of the law point the need not for the rejection, but for the reappraisal, of the legal system. Only if the reappraisal fails to produce an acceptable answer, should we embark on the unknown, but deeply suspect, waters of a vital human activity, developing outside the control of the general law.*

It is precisely because we have sailed on those waters for so long that we ran into the Grunwick storm. This needs to be spelled out. It was said in the early part of this book that it was an act of moral principle for APEX to take on the case of the Grunwick strikers. If they wanted a union they should be entitled to have one. Their case was weakened by the fact that the first strikers left the company (Mrs Desai resigned; Devshi Bhudia provoked a quarrel having found another job) before joining a union and only sought one when it might be said that they were trying to extricate themselves from troubles of their own making. But they can be forgiven for this lapse from normal trade union good practice on the ground that they could not be expected to know better, being recent immigrants. That said, the subsequent behaviour of the trade union movement became less defensible as it became more extra-legal, and it was at its most reprehensible when the unions took to the streets.

* *English Law, The New Dimension*, London, Stevens & Sons, 1974.

Wait a minute, it will be protested; they had no option. Grunwick was immovable. The law could not provide justice. The union had to use other means. But why was the law inadequate? The answer is to be found in the union movement's own reluctance to have anything to do with the law. Let us summarize what this has meant in the Grunwick case.

Because of union reluctance to have the courts debate the merits of industrial disputes the strikers could not go to an industrial tribunal to argue the case for reinstatement. Because of union reluctance to accept detailed written rules affecting their interests ACAS could be taken through the courts for a year or more, as the company sought to have its recommendation declared null and void. Because of union insistence on a minimum of written rules in the Act establishing ACAS Grunwick had every incentive to defend itself in the courts. Because of trade union insistence on the legalization of the closed shop the workers at Grunwick who did not want to join a union, especially after their experiences at the hands of the pickets, could not be guaranteed protection against future demands that they become members of APEX – whatever APEX may have promised, in all good faith, during the development of the dispute. Because of police opposition, and TUC reluctance to accept written rules, the law of picketing was in a muddle, making the demonstrations and mass pickets harder to control. And the way Grunwick saw it, because the law is written to suit the unions, its opponents could make libellous or slanderous accusations about the conditions in the factory (later shown by the Scarman report to be highly exaggerated) without any legal defence being open to the company.

This absence of any clearly stated code of laws setting out both the rights and the responsibilities of trade unions is the most glaring omission in current British law, weakening the protection that our constitution can offer to trade unions, companies, individual workers, and indeed all citizens, and consequently damaging our economy. Again Sir Leslie Scarman's 1974 lectures provide the necessary quotation: 'It is perhaps too often forgotten,' he said then, 'that one of the merits of the rule of law is that it is a curb upon power — irrespective of the person or institution who wields it.'

Trade unions may be right when they say that a court cannot settle arguments about wages, or holidays, or hours of work, although many courts of arbitration have done so in the past. In that sense 'keeping the law out of industrial disputes' may have some merit. But when it comes to rules that ensure that the unions treat their own members fairly, or that they do not bully people who do not wish to be union members, or that in their 'industrial action' they understand the agreed law and pay the penalty if there is a breach, there is no question that in these and many similar areas the trade union movement should accept the discipline of law. Most people, including most trade unionists, have shown through opinion polls that they support this view. Some Government, perhaps in the not too distant future, will have to grasp this nettle again, and extend the law to delineate the ground-rules of trade union behaviour.

People will say, 'That is impossible.' Ask why, and the answer will be 'The unions will not accept it.' This is the fatal defect in modern British society: that because the strongest extra-legal force will not accept the same obedience to general rules as all other sections of society, the adverse consequences must simply be accepted, with a shrug of the shoulders.

Is not the purpose of this book to rehearse the economic arguments that have arisen from the Grunwick dispute. But it should be mentioned that the absence of generally agreed rules has damaging effects on the economy. For example, small businesses should provide the dynamism that might move the sluggish economy forwards again. Yet it is these small companies that rightly or wrongly feel threatened by new laws making it difficult for them to dismiss workers they take on, costly to maintain workers they keep, and dangerous to exist at all if they or their employees wish to deny the entrance of a trade union into their affairs. At Grunwick the willing workers rode the company bus every day through a barrage of jeers and catcalls from the strikers, yet in spite of that the Scarman report seemed to imply that their interests (and they were in the majority) were of less value than the interests of those on strike.

165

Small businessmen see this, and wonder just where they stand with the law, at a time when trade unions are actively seeking to enrol their workers.

Only a clear set of rules can end the damage created by these vague fears and uncertainties. These rules need not favour recalcitrant employers; ideally they should provide for trade union recognition where the workers show by ballot that they want it. They should set out what actions unions might legally take, and what actions are against the law – in letter, spirit, meaning and intent. The rights and obligations of employers and those who choose not to join unions should also be codified, as should the rules affecting the treatment of individual members by the unions they belong to. Such a set of laws would be a tremendous change in British practice; some people might argue that it would not be possible to make them work unless there was a new constitutional settlement. Is this too much to ask for? That Sir Leslie Scarman – Lord Scarman – in his 1974 lectures included among his 'tentative proposals':

(1) A new constitutional settlement replacing that of 1689 to be worked out by Parliament, the judges, the Law Commissions, and the Government through a phased programme of study, research, and extensive consultation;
(2) The basis of the new settlement should be entrenched provisions (including a Bill of Rights), and restraint upon administrative and legislative power, protecting it from attack by a bare majority in Parliament;
(3) A Supreme Court of the United Kingdom charged with the duty of protecting the Constitution . . .

Of course Sir Leslie Scarman was not in those lectures thinking exclusively or even primarily of industrial relations legislation; he had in mind such matters as the retreat of the common law as new statutes multiplied, the possibility of the establishment of devolved Parliaments in Scotland and Wales, and the like. But industrial relations law played an important part in his lecture, as can be seen from the passage quoted on pages 162 and 163.

The general arguments for and against a broad new constitutional settlement are outside the scope of this book. But whether there is such a development or not, a new settlement of the part of our law and constitution affecting trade union rights and responsibilities is urgent. Young Devshi Bhudia may not have thought of any of this on that hot Friday in August 1976, but it is the central, and most fundamental, lesson of the long dispute that started with his walk-out.

Appendices

The chronology

The following list includes most of the main events. Some subsidiary events, such as small court cases, have been omitted. Some related events, such as the proposed boycott of mail to South Africa, are included.

AUGUST 1976

20 August   Morning: George Ward, managing director of Grunwick, leaves for Ireland on holiday.

Early afternoon: Devshi Bhudia and three or four other young men leave Grunwick mail-order department.

Late afternoon: Mrs Desai and her son, Sunil, walk out.

23 August   Morning: first pickets out early, bearing crude home-made placards. Sunil Desai bicycles off to the Citizens' Advice Bureau to find a trade union. Speaks on telephone to Len Gristey, London area organizer of APEX, who promises a meeting the following evening.

3 o'clock: mass walk-out at Chapter Road; march round to Cobbold Road where about 25 other workers join the strike. Riot. Police called. Company later says there was vandalism and damage at Cobbold Road. By end of day some 65 employees (30 of them students) on strike.

24 August   Jack Dromey, Secretary of Brent Trades Council, meets strikers at about 11 a.m. Addresses them at Trades Hall that evening. Arranges for them to elect a committee. Then withdraws as Len Gristey enrols about 60 new members in APEX.

26 August   Atmosphere tense. Gristey meets Stacey, personnel manager of Grunwick, and Pearson, a director, on pavement outside company office. They fail to understand one another. Gristey undertakes to write to Grunwick board.

27 August   Gristey writes his letter, asking for a meeting.

31 August   Roy Grantham, General Secretary of APEX, returns to his office in Wimbledon to find a report from Gristey on his desk. He seeks more information. Gristey, meanwhile, telephones to chase Grunwick.

ACAS, by now told of dispute, offers to convene a joint meeting; Grunwick declines. APEX declares strike 'official'. Number on strike now 137, of which 46 are students.

SEPTEMBER 1976

1 September   ACAS offers services to management.

2 September   Strikers sacked by Grunwick.
Hickey, for Grunwick, replies to Gristey letter of 27 August, informing him of sackings.
ACAS tries again; Grunwick says no again.

6 September   Ward returns from holiday.

7 September   Grantham addresses annual conference of TUC, asks for support in Grunwick dispute.

8 September   Gristey writes another letter asking for a meeting.

9 September   Meeting of Grunwick joint works committee. Complaints about wages, holidays, sickness benefit. Reference to attitude of managers which had changed noticeably (for the better) 'during the past few weeks', according to later APEX gloss on the minutes.

10 September   ACAS offers assistance to management; turned down.

14 September   Grantham asks Tom Jackson, General Secretary of the Union of Post Office Workers, for help.

20 September   Non-committal reply from Grunwick to Gristey's letter of 8 September.

23 September   Reg Freeson, Labour MP for Brent East, writes to Grunwick, asks them to reconsider.

30 September   ACAS offers its services to management; turned down.

OCTOBER 1976

5 October   Grantham asks Secretary of State for Employment, Albert Booth, to set up court of inquiry into dispute.

7 October Len Murray, General Secretary of TUC, asks unions to give 'all possible assistance' to APEX, including blacking of Grunwick's services.

15 October Booth turns down Grantham request for court of inquiry. Prefers to wait and see if ACAS can work it out. Grantham officially asks ACAS to take on the union's claim to recognition by Grunwick, under Section 11 of Employment Protection Act.

19 October ACAS tries to meet Grunwick. Managing director not available.

21 October Grunwick phones to say that it is sending written reply to ACAS.

25 October ACAS phones Grunwick, unable to contact managing director.

Finance and General Purposes Committee of TUC discusses dispute. Agree that Tom Jackson and Len Murray will meet to talk about possible Post Office blacking of Grunwick's mail.

At 6.15 p.m. Ward approaches John Gorst, MP for Hendon North; he subsequently becomes unpaid public relations adviser to company and its managing director.

26 October ACAS meets Grunwick for first time. Finds prospect of a conciliated settlement 'not encouraging'. But company says it would cooperate in an inquiry.

NOVEMBER 1976

1 November Post Office workers at Cricklewood sorting office refuse to receive or release Grunwick mailbags.

National Association for Freedom takes up case. Grunwick meets ACAS again, says again it would cooperate in inquiry – but if Post Office blacking was not stopped company would be obliged to close down and there could not be an inquiry.

2 November John Gorst, Conservative MP for Hendon North, forces brief debate in Commons.

3 November Tom Jackson tells ACAS his union will call off blacking at Cricklewood, if company will accept procedures of ACAS on recognition.

Grunwick meets ACAS, says it would cooperate in the inquiry.

Jackson tells Grantham and Gristey he is calling off blacking.

4 November Emergency debate in the Commons. First full airing of issues in dispute. Sponsored by NAFF, Grunwick applies to High Court for injunction against Union of Post Office Workers' action at Cricklewood. Post Office and UPW named as defendants.

UPW officially ends blacking of Grunwick mail.

8 November High Court action against UPW abandoned.

ACAS meets APEX to plan survey of workers' opinion.

10 November ACAS meets Grunwick, which challenges plan to send questionnaire to strikers because, says Grunwick, they had been dismissed several weeks before approach to ACAS for recognition.

17 November ACAS hands Grunwick form of proposed questionnaire to study; Grunwick says it will take legal advice. Agrees to give names of employees, says ACAS.

22 November ACAS phones Grunwick to ask for a meeting and is told letter is being drafted following legal advice; there could be no meeting until company had had a reply.

25 November Grunwick increases wages by 15 per cent 'across the board'.

26 November No letter received. 'Repeated inquiries abortive,' says ACAS.

27 November Company sends letter setting out technical points in dispute.

30 November ACAS receives letter, sends interim reply by hand same day and further reply on 2 December.

DECEMBER 1976

3 December ACAS unable to contact Grunwick on phone.

7 December ACAS phones again; offered meeting on 10 December.

10 December ACAS meets Grunwick. Objections on two points remain unresolved. Company arranging further legal advice.

12 December Len Murray challenges Conservative Party to 'stand up and be counted in situations like Grunwicks'.

13 December Weekend report that UPW will renew blacking of post if there is no progress in Grunwick–ACAS talks.

174

15 December ACAS told by Grunwick, on telephone, that company could not meet their legal advisers (because of the lawyers' other commitments) before 21 December. ACAS asks for meeting on 22 December.

Report that executive council of UPW had instructed Tom Jackson to 'keep a close watch on the situation' at Grunwick.

16 December Another phone call. ACAS told by Grunwick there could be no meeting on 22 or 23 December. Company closed for holiday from 24 December to 3 January inclusive. Could meet from 4 January onwards.

17 December Yet another request to Grunwick for meeting before Christmas proved unsuccessful, says ACAS. 'We considered this further delay unreasonable and determined to proceed with the inquiry without the cooperation of the employer.'

20 December Brief adjournment debate on Grunwick, on motion of Mr Ted Fletcher, Labour MP for Darlington.

29 December ACAS sends questionnaires and covering letters to APEX members; most are strikers, but a few still work inside Grunwicks.

JANUARY 1977

5 January ACAS sends out more questionnaires, and again the following day. Total dispatched: 110.

13 January Meanwhile, in Brussels, International Confederation of Free Trade Unions had called for international trade union action against South Africa, in protest at apartheid policies. UPW had announced its support.

In the Commons Secretary of State for Industry, Eric Varley, says 'it is far too premature at this stage to comment on the situation'.

14 January John Gouriet, administrative director of NAFF, asks Sam Silkin, QC, Attorney-General, to permit proceedings to be taken in his name against the unions, so that the Post Office boycott can be stopped. Silkin refuses. Gouriet goes to High Court. His application turned down by Mr Justice Stocker.

15 January Lord Denning, Master of the Rolls, sits on Saturday to hear appeal; boycott is due to begin on Monday. Appeal upheld; boycott banned. Court rebukes Silkin.

18 January   Silkin tells Appeal Court it had no right to challenge his decision.

20 January   Foot defends Silkin in Commons.

21 January   While indirectly related Post Office case rumbles on, Grantham tells Ward that APEX will submit claim for fair wages under Employment Protection Act.

27 January   Mixed decision by Appeal Court; severe criticism of Silkin. (Case eventually goes to House of Lords.)

29 January   Grunwick strikers picket chemists' shops.

FEBRUARY 1977

10 February   ACAS sends out draft copies of its report, proposing recognition of APEX by company.

17 February   APEX accepts this.

21 February   TUC Finance and General Purposes Committee debates Post Office case at length; agrees to support PO unions' appeal to House of Lords.

25 February   Market and Opinion Research International canvasses opinions of employees still within Grunwick. Questionnaires completed: 250. Result: for negotiation of pay and conditions by a trade union 21 (8·4 per cent); for existing (non-trade union) system at Grunwick 216 (86·4 per cent); don't know 13 (5·2 per cent).

MARCH 1977

7 March   Grantham says he will ask TUC for coordinated action to cut off all supplies and services to Grunwick.

10 March   ACAS publishes its final report. Questionnaires completed: 93; for APEX: 93; members of APEX replying: 93. ACAS recommends recognition of APEX by Grunwick. Company says it will go to court to have report declared void.

21 March   By permission, Roy Grantham addresses regular meeting of TUC Finance and General Purposes Committee. Asks for statement by General Council of TUC condemning company and pledging support of trade union movement, and continued blacking of Grunwick products and services. Before Grantham enters meeting, committee debates progress on Post Office unions' appeal to House of Lords. TUC agrees to meet one third of any costs incurred.

23 March Fifty-nine dismissed strikers complain of unfair dismissal. North London Industrial tribunal rules that it has no jurisdiction in the case.

APRIL 1977

1 April Grunwick increases wages by 10 per cent 'across the board'.

MAY 1977

15 May On eve of annual conference of Union of Post Office Workers Eric Varley writes to Tom Jackson promising to amend Post and Telegraph Acts, so as to affirm right of trade unions representing Post Office workers to strike.

Speaking at conference deputy leader of Labour Party, Michael Foot, says Post Office workers had had their rights 'filched away from them'. He adds: 'if the freedom of the people of this country – and especially the rights of trade unionists – had been left to the good sense and fair-mindedness of judges, we would have precious few freedoms in this country'.

19 May Shirley Williams, Education Secretary, Fred Mulley, Defence Secretary, and Denis Howell, Sports Minister (and President of APEX), join Grunwick picket line. Shown on TV.

Unconfirmed report that Prime Minister subsequently told his Cabinet not to join picket lines without his approval.

23 May TUC Finance and General Purposes Committee hears report that Sam Silkin had confirmed in talk with Len Murray that Post Office case being pursued by NAFF could have considerable dangers for trade unions. If Lords decided that individuals could initiate and pursue cases to extent of securing an interim injunction (as had been done through Lord Denning's Saturday court), Government would want to introduce amending legislation.

After the mass picketing began on 13 June, four weeks of national attention to a previously small, local dispute followed.

Week 1 **13 June** 'One-week' mass picket in Chapter Road and Cobbold Road. Police arrest 84 pickets. Newspapers and television rush reporters to the scene. Maximum number of police: 308. Estimated (by police) maximum number of pickets: 700.

14 June Company brings employees to work by bus, to take them through mass picket line. 13 pickets arrested. Police: 503; pickets (say police) 700. Both 'peak hour' figures.

15 June Postal workers at Cricklewood vote to ban Grunwick mail. Blacking not official.
 Scotland Yard says it will investigate allegations that police have used undue force.
 Police: 356; pickets: 700 at morning 'peak hour'.

16 June Grantham enters factory. Addresses employees; shouted down. Six pickets arrested. Maximum on line: 521 police; 700 pickets.

17 June APEX decides to continue mass picketing, writes to TUC asking again for support from General Council.
 Grunwick considers suing postal workers. Silkin rejects demand for legal action against them.
 Police, 688; pickets, 1,500 at 'peak hour'.

18 June Booth asks Grantham, Ward and Jim Mortimer, Chairman of ACAS, to meet him at Department of Employment. Message reaches Ward, by telephone, at 7 p.m.

19 June 7 p.m. Ward is telephoned again; Booth offers to meet him separately from APEX. Ward says Booth should come to meet him at Grunwicks.

Week 2 **20 June** In Cricklewood, Monday morning starts with 556 police and 1,200 pickets.
 At Congress House TUC Finance and General Purposes Committee meets. Notes that Grantham had during previous week repeated his request to Booth for a court of inquiry. Grantham letter of 17 June asking for TUC support circulated to committee members.
 In House of Commons, short debate following previous week's highly publicized picketing.

In House of Lords, Post Office unions' appeal against Denning judgement begins.

Up north, miners decide to join picket line.

From Grunwick, Ward challenges Silkin to act over unlawful picketing.

At Department of Employment, St James's Square, effort to bring Ward to meet Booth intensifies. Six telephone calls to and from Grunwick between 4.40 p.m. and 7.10 p.m. No luck. Booth meets Grantham and Mortimer anyway.

21 June Audrey Wise, Labour MP for Coventry South-West, arrested on picket line. Seven other left-wing Labour MPs on line. Police present: 765; pickets, 1,000 at busiest time.

Ward writes to Booth saying he would meet him at Grunwick. Booth replies repeating invitation to Ward to come and meet him.

On Callaghan's instructions, Rees chairs first meeting of *ad hoc* Cabinet committee to oversee dispute. Members: Rees, Booth, Silkin, and later, Varley. Place: Rees's room in Commons, formerly Mrs Thatcher's office. Ministers debate Prime Minister's request to limit number of pickets.

22 June General Council of TUC discusses APEX request for more help. 'This is a matter of principle,' says Hugh Scanlon. Council urges member unions to 'intensify their financial and practical aid to those on strike'.

Letter from Department of Employment to Ward invites him to come in later that day to meet Booth. At 6.40 p.m. Ward telephones to say he and his adviser could come the following day. Meeting fixed for 3 p.m.

Rees committee arranges talks between Grantham and senior Scotland Yard officer to arrange better control of picket lines. Plans made by same Cabinet committee to have High Court hearing of Ward's case against ACAS brought forward.

Picket line scuffles increase.

Mrs Margaret Thatcher issues statement asking Prime Minister to 'state categorically' that police have full backing of Government.

Government anxiety mounts as headlines blacken.

Maximum number of police: 631; pickets, 800. Arrests to date: 189.

23 June Two coachloads of coal-miners from Barnsley drive through night to join picket line, led by Arthur Scargill. Scottish miners led by Mick McGahey also on their way. Scargill arrested.

PC Trevor Wilson injured in clashes outside company gates; picture of him lying prone after being hit by flying bottle regarded by all parties as most emotionally powerful image of street struggle.

In Commons, Silkin says he has asked Post Office what steps it has taken to have mail delivered in Cricklewood.

Ward, with Gorst, Hickey (a director of Grunwick) and his legal adviser (Robins), meet Booth in his office. Booth asks Ward his views on a court of inquiry; Ward says he will be bound by the courts alone. No agreement reached.

Grantham has meeting at Scotland Yard; use of armbands by official pickets suggested. Callaghan associated himself with idea.

ACAS asks Lord Chief Justice to bring forward hearing; it is fixed for 4 July.

Police: 793; pickets 2,000 (peak hour figures).

24 June A BLOT ON BRITAIN says *Daily Mail* headline, with most of front page devoted to pictures of PC Wilson. Commissioner of Police, David McNee, goes to hospital to visit Wilson. Rees committee meets, debates powers of police. Booth tells it TUC statement of two days previously was so phrased as to dissuade miners from coming down in overwhelming numbers. He was continuing with mediation.

Booth writes to Grantham and Ward proposing to appoint independent mediator. Grantham accepts.

Police: 1,521; demonstrators: 2,200.

25 June Silkin at Anglo-American seminar on 'The News and the Law' at Hythe. Scarman also present. Silkin summoned to Chequers.

26 June Rees group meets at Chequers, under the chairmanship of the Prime Minister. Callaghan's anxieties made known. Committee agrees to consider urgently setting up court of inquiry. Private attempts to be made to persuade postmen to return to work. In public statement Booth says he had asked his private secretary to contact Ward; Ward dictates letter in which he says he will not be bound by mediation.

Week 3 **27 June** Monday morning: 1,356 police; 900 pickets at peak hour.

Home Secretary Rees visits factory. Cheered by crowd outside gates.

Booth and Ward meet; Ward says he could not agree in advance to accept mediator's judgement. Rees committee sets its officials to work to prepare paper on setting up court of inquiry. Name of Lord Justice Scarman mentioned.

28 June London District Council of Union of Post Office Workers

180

votes to apply Cricklewood ban on Grunwick mail throughout London. Tom Jackson says this cannot be made official by UPW executive 'as it is illegal under 1953 PO Act'.

Grantham meets strike committee, writes to General Secretaries of other unions asking for large numbers of pickets to join line on a regular basis.

National 'day of action' due on 11 July backed by miners' unions.

In the Commons, Rees says that so far 95 police officers have received minor injuries, and two 'more serious' injuries. Rees committee discusses court of inquiry. Booth still reluctant to arrange one until mediation attempts seen to be finally dead.

Police on the line: 1,338.

29 June Booth still tries for mediation; APEX will not call off mass pickets if Grunwick will not agree to accept result. Deadlock. Later Booth discusses court of inquiry with Grantham; Post Office action with Jackson.

Notices posted in London sorting offices asking staff to work normally or be sent home without pay.

In Rees committee, Ministers decide that announcement about Court of Inquiry should be made following day, to cool tempers and restore 'law and order'.

Tactics for emergency debate in Commons discussed.

APEX tries to persuade relevant unions to cut off water and electricity supplies to Grunwick. Fails.

Police on line 615.

30 June Booth announces setting up of Scarman Inquiry.

Heated emergency debate in Commons. Silkin still opposed to prosecution of postmen blacking Grunwick mail.

Police 746.

JULY 1977

1 July Court of Inquiry private meeting; decision to hold first hearing on 5 July. APEX says blacking of supplies to Grunwick will continue, as will peaceful picketing. Attention focused on mass march by trade unionists through Willesden on 11 July. Atmosphere on picket line less heated.

Week 4 **4 July** Grunwick appeal against ACAS decision opens in High Court.

Rees committee meets, looks to arrangements for 11 July. Agree that priority is to get unions to talk to police as soon as possible.

5 July Court of Inquiry opens formally; adjourns until 11 July to give High Court chance to complete ACAS case.

Post Office starts suspending without pay employees at Cricklewood who refuse to handle Grunwick mail. No mail delivered in NW2.

6 July Rees committee hears that APEX and TUC cooperating well with each other and police; Scargill and Brent Trades Council being awkward.

7 July Rees committee hears TUC has brought Scargill under official strike committee and TUC control.

10 July NAFF helps take Grunwick mail to be posted in country postboxes. A Saturday midnight coup.

11 July A Monday of 'mass action'. Police arrest 69 pickets; 18 police injured. Crowd estimated at 18,000. Police present: 3,706. As on other days, no accurate estimate of numbers of pickets or demonstrators hurt. Incidents ugly; march nevertheless mainly peaceful and controlled by TUC.

Rees committee meets at midday to hear reports from field.

Rees makes statement in Commons, 'we dissociate ourselves from all acts of violence, from wherever they come'. Scarman Inquiry begins taking evidence from APEX.

(At this point the division of the chronology by weeks ceases.)

12 July High Court verdict: victory for ACAS over Grunwick.

Callaghan asks both sides to accept this. Brief exchanges in Commons and Lords.

13 July APEX and its Grunwick strike committee agree statement that 'no further demonstrations, marches or large-scale picketing will be held during the period of the Court of Inquiry'.

Number of police on picket line down to 215 at peak. Number arrested since 13 June: 377. Number of police injured so far: 243. Other injuries, e.g. to crowds: unknown.

14 July Len Murray circularizes APEX statement; accompanying letter attempts to channel help by affiliated unions strictly through APEX.

Cricklewood company tries to get High Court to order Post Office to hand over mail locked in sorting office. Fails.

18 July Appeal against High Court decision of 14 June, on PO mail, turned down.

182

20 July Secret ballot by Gallup Poll organization at Grunwick factory results in 85 per cent vote against any trade union negotiating pay and conditions.

Postal workers refuse to handle 20,000 Grunwick packages.

23 July Post Office allows Grunwick to retrieve 65 mailbags from Cricklewood; orders re-opening of sorting office from following day.

25 July Post Office workers return, but are immediately locked out again for refusing to handle Grunwick mail.

Varley says that Post Office had suggested suspending its monopoly over mail deliveries, but that Cabinet had said no.

26 July Victory for Silkin in House of Lords: Denning judgement against him overturned in case of Gouriet v. Post Office Unions over blacking of mail to South Africa.

27 July Scarman inquiry completes taking of evidence in public; retires to consider verdict.

29 July Appeal Court overturns High Court decision on ACAS; finds in favour of Grunwick.

Postmen decide to end blacking of Grunwick mail.

APEX forces its strike committee to cancel mass picket originally scheduled for 8 August.

'Black Friday', say militant supporters of strikers.

AUGUST 1977

1 August ACAS decides to take Appeal Court verdict to House of Lords.

6 August Seven dismissed van drivers fail to win reinstatement.

8 August Peaceful mass demonstration and picket. No injuries. No arrests. Police appear to outnumber pickets.

12 August A thousand letters sent by strike committee to mobilize support for post-Scarman action.

19 August Strike committee asks APEX and TGWU to put an emergency resolution on the agenda of the TUC conference calling for all supplies and services to Grunwicks to be cut off.

23 August SE region of TUC conference passes similar resolution.

25 August   Scarman report published, recommending re-employment of all strikers who were full-time workers at plant, plus recognition of a union.

30 August   Grantham offers 'compromise' to Grunwick: phased reinstatement of strikers; guarantee of no closed shop; arbitration in future disputes if APEX is recognized.

31 August   Ward rejects principal recommendations of Scarman report, accepting only that individual workers should be represented by trade unions if they so wish. 'Never, in any circumstances will the company reinstate those who were, very properly, dismissed.'

APEX, TUC, Brent Trades Council, and strike committee all indicate their determination to intensify the struggle.

The Scarman conclusions

The conclusions and recommendations of this report are reproduced below. The numbers refer to paragraph numbers in the report.

Conclusions

65. The underlying cause of the walk-out on 23 August 1976 was a genuine, even if not clearly formulated, sense of discontent and grievance amongst a substantial number of staff – particularly in the mail-order department. The demand for a union, which was the cry of those who went on strike, summed up accurately their sense of grievance: they wanted some body independent of management with the knowledge to advise them and the strength to make some impact upon the company.

66. Their discontent and grievances arose from the company's lack of a properly developed industrial relations policy including effective machinery for the examination and redress of grievances.

67. The company by dismissing all the strikers, refusing to consider the reinstatement of any of them, refusing to seek a negotiated settlement to the strike and rejecting ACAS offers of conciliation, has acted within the letter but outside the spirit of the law. Further, such action on the part of the company was unreasonable when judged by the norms of good industrial relations practice. The company has thus added to the bitterness of the dispute, and contributed to its development into a threat of civil disorder.

68. Once the recognition issue was referred to ACAS by the union, the company recognized that by law it must cooperate with ACAS in its inquiries. It is not for us to pass judgement on the legal differences which arose between the company and ACAS: nor are we in a position to determine whether the company 'dragged its heels' or ACAS was justified in deciding on 20 December to proceed without the assistance of the company. We merely note that the company has exercised its

undoubted right of access to the courts to test the validity of the ACAS report, and that the consequent legal proceedings have added to the delays which have so greatly embittered the dispute.

69. The union acted reasonably in responding to the strikers' call for help, in enrolling them as members and in seeking to negotiate with the company. When the strikers were dismissed, the union had no choice but to add a claim for their reinstatement to its existing claim to be recognized by the company for the purpose of collective bargaining.

70. In all the circumstances the union was fully justified in raising the dispute at the Trades Union Congress and invoking the support of the trade union movement as a whole. It was also fully justified in referring on 15 October 1976 a recognition issue to ACAS.

71. The union, however, when frustrated by the seemingly indefinite prolongation of the dispute in 1977, in calling for further industrial action by members of the UPW took a step which led to breaches of the criminal law. Although it was never the intention of the union the mass picket on occasion had led to forms of civil disorder. It could have been foreseen that this was likely.

72. In our judgement, good industrial relations depend upon a willingness to cooperate and compromise. The law favours collective bargaining and encourages the use by workers of independent trade unions for the purpose. The policy of the law is to exclude 'trade disputes' from judicial review by the courts and to rely not on the compulsory processes of the law but on the voluntary approach backed by advice, conciliation, and arbitration to promote good industrial relations. The efficacy of such a law depends upon good will. If men act unreasonably, by which we mean in obedience to the letter but not the spirit of the law, it will not work. It does not, however, follow that judicial review would be an effective substitute: for whatever the sanctions imposed by law, its efficacy depends upon the consent of the people.

Recommendations

73. (1) Reinstatement

In the conduct of industrial relations in this country, and no matter what the legalities are, it is the exception rather than the rule for employees who are dismissed during the course of a strike not to be re-engaged after the dispute is ended. Ideally in our view Grunwick should therefore offer re-employment to all those strikers who before the dispute were full-time employees of the company and who wish to be taken back. It is our recommendation that this should be done if it be at all practicable. We recognize however that the nature of the company's business is such that the necessary number of vacancies may not now exist, although it seems to us that a seasonal business dependent on overtime must have at least some vacancies.

In the absence of any established relationship between Grunwick and APEX the question of determining the number of vacancies which do exist could well, and we recommend should, be considered by a mediator either agreed by the company and the union, or appointed by the Secretary of State for Employment in the absence of such agreement.

It would in our opinion be reasonable for the company to make to those for whom there are no vacancies, an *ex gratia* payment commensurate with their length of service. The amounts of such payments are a matter on which the mediator might well be able to offer helpful advice.

(2) Individual rights of representation

We were pleased to hear it said on behalf of the company during the course of our inquiry that if an individual employee who was a member of the union had a grievance which he or she could not settle directly with the management, and wished to be represented by the union in pursuance of that grievance, the company would accept that right. We recommend that the company give effect to this declaration.

(3) Recognition for the purposes of collective bargaining

Whatever the result of the company's case against ACAS (which is now for the House of Lords to decide), ACAS is the body established by law to determine the recognition issue in the absence of agreement. We do not propose to pre-judge the issue. Nevertheless, we have no doubt that union representation, if properly encouraged and responsibly exercised, could in the future help the company as well as its employees.

(4) Law reform

We are not a suitable body to propose specific reforms of the law: nor do our terms of reference enable us to make the sort of inquiries necessary for the formulation of sound proposals. And, of course, we are not able to engage in consultations – the very stuff of law reform.

The report also welcomed the Government's announcement in an answer in the House of Commons on 12 July that the Government has under review the law relating to picketing.

Mr Ward's Reply

The statement issued by Grunwick on 31 August 1977 reads as follows:

The scope of the Scarman Inquiry

When the Secretary of State for Employment, using the powers conferred upon him by Section 4 of the Industrial Courts Act 1919, established an Inquiry headed by the Rt Hon Lord Justice Scarman OBE, with Mr J. P. Lowry and Mr T. Parry CBE, OBE, as the other members, he directed that the terms of reference to the Court should be as follows:

'To inquire into the causes and circumstances of, and relevant to, the dispute, other than any matter before the High Court, until the final determination of those proceedings, and to report.'

This was in itself a very peculiar remit, because few concerned citizens could have been unaware that Grunwick was in dispute with former employees whom it had dismissed and who were represented by APEX. Fewer still could have failed to notice the course the dispute had taken. To follow its instructions, all the Court of Inquiry needed to do was to reproduce newspaper coverage of the dispute, which would have informed the Secretary of State of all that had happened and the differing standpoints of the protagonists.

Of course nobody supposed that the Court of Inquiry had so restricted a function. It had been established for a political purpose. It took no evidence from witnesses on oath, and because it was in haste to produce a report, limited the number of witnesses it heard. Its job was to resolve a dispute which was embarrassing the Government. It had no power to make any orders which were legally enforceable (unlike a normal Court which operates within clearly laid down rules and which can make legally enforceable orders which are subject to appeal).

Grunwick was therefore, from the outset, presented with a difficult

189

choice. The Government was not an impartial observer of the dispute. It had given complete backing to APEX. In all discussions with Grunwick management the Government had urged it to capitulate to the strikers. Three Government ministers had joined the APEX picket line outside Grunwick. It was beyond belief that a Government committed so completely to APEX had established an Inquiry that it thought would produce a report hostile to that trade Union's interests.

On the other hand, if Grunwick refused to cooperate with the Court of Inquiry, the wider political purposes for which the Inquiry had been set up would at once be discounted. It would be claimed that the only function of the Inquiry was to determine the causes and circumstances of the dispute. By refusing cooperation, Grunwick would be held to be afraid to have such causes and circumstances investigated. That in turn would be transformed into an admission that the extravagant calumnies put abroad by APEX and the strikers were true.

Another consideration affected Grunwick's decision to cooperate. The Company had little doubt that any Inquiry would reject the APEX version of how the strike started. Even if the recommendations bore little relation to the evidence, the demolition of a carefully constructed edifice of falsehood, which had gained widespread currency because of constant repetition, must have an impact on public opinion.

Grunwick therefore offered the Court of Inquiry its complete cooperation in determining the causes and circumstances of the dispute and fulfilling its instructions from the Secretary of State. But Grunwick refused to be bound by any recommendations the Inquiry might make.

Grunwick believes the wisdom of the course of action it took will be apparent to those who read the report of the Court of Inquiry. The evidence, as expected, favours Grunwick. The recommendations, as expected, do not.

The philosophy of the report of the Court of Inquiry

Before commenting in detail on the Report, Grunwick thinks it will be helpful to explain its attitude towards the philosophy that lies behind the Report.

It is not a philosophy based upon malice, nor upon a desire to sanctify an injustice. Put baldly, it is the philosophy of the Corporate State. The Report does not of course claim that English Law has yet benefited from the legislation needed to sustain a corporate state and that Grunwick are lawbreakers for defying such enactments. On the contrary, the Report makes constant references to Grunwick's scrupulous observance of the law and praises the Company for this. But the praise is qualified by an occasional reference to the 'letter of the law', and there are several references to the 'spirit of the law', or even more vaguely to the 'policy of the law'. Grunwick is held to have behaved according to the 'letter of the law', but somehow to have fallen short of apprehending the niceties of 'the policy of the law', as the Government and powerful vested interests would wish that policy to be.

But when this 'policy of the law' is examined, it turns out to have nothing to do with law of any description and everything to do with conciliating the trade unions. It is the Trade Unions themselves who have most strenuously insisted that as little law as possible be applied to trade disputes. They have been unwilling to allow the law in these matters to become coherent, or to apply to a whole range of cases that are of daily occurrence in British Industry. Their assumption has been that the law would compel them to honour bargains and regulate their activities in a way they find uncongenial, or adverse to their interests. Thus it is a very strong argument that arrives at the conclusion that where the law is not on the side of the trade unions, businessmen owe it to the community to interpret it as if it were.

Such an assumption is in every way appropriate to a corporate state, where individuals consent to, or are compelled to consent to, having their interests represented by associations. In such a state, Government, employers' associations, and trade unions decide what industrial policy should be. Individuals are not allowed to disturb the symmetry of these arrangements by any inconvenient appeal to natural rights. The group decides for the individual. If any additional legal force is required to coerce the recalcitrant, a new enactment, often with retrospective provisions, is passed in short order.

Though Britain has been moving towards these tripartite arrangements, they have not yet been given the force of law, or indeed of popular approval. Unfortunately the Report of the Court of Inquiry tends to underplay this fact. It takes no account of the wishes of the existing Grunwick workforce, because it equates workers' best interests with trade union representation. It believes that Grunwick has sometimes acted 'unreasonably', because a refusal to accommodate the desires of a Government and trade unions, especially when no approval for such a refusal is sought from any trade association, obviously struck the three members of the Court of Inquiry as perverse.

Grunwick wishes to make it clear that it claims the right to dissent from corporatist political assumptions. Perhaps Britain would be happier if the individual had less freedom, though Grunwick does not think so. But it is a matter for the British people as a whole through their representatives in Parliament and not for Courts of Inquiry. So long as an area of freedom still exists, a good citizen has every right to enjoy it. He ought not to be dissuaded by being told that the exercise of his undoubted rights is irritating powerful groups, who desire him to act in a manner better suited to the advancement of their interests.

The start of the dispute

Grunwick has little to contest in the Report's explanation of how the dispute began, except that the Court of Inquiry nowhere gives sufficient weight to the evidence it accepts.

The dispute began when Mr Devshi Bhudia, aged nineteen, walked off the job. From the start, Grunwick maintained that this was a premeditated action by someone who had nothing to lose and whose only concern was to cause an industrial dispute. This has repeatedly been denied and various fanciful accounts of what occurred have gained currency. But the Report puts the matter quite clearly.

'There was an element of predetermination in Mr Bhudia's departure. He had become discontented with pay and conditions and a week earlier had discussed with some the possibility of joining a union. He had carried his dissatisfaction sufficiently far to seek and obtain the promise of a job elsewhere before, *on his own admission*, he provoked the incident which brought about his dismissal.'

That should establish beyond doubt that Mr Bhudia wanted to be dismissed and the question that arises is why? Again the Report very clearly explains the facts – facts which Grunwick has been asserting and the strikers denying since the beginning of the dispute.

Mrs Jayaben Desai, who subsequently became the strike leader, was not dismissed at all. As the Report says 'There was an altercation and Mrs Desai asked for her cards and walked out.'

But Mrs Desai, who had asked for her cards, and Mr Bhudia, who found another job and then contrived his own dismissal, did not leave the matter there. On the following Monday morning they were outside Grunwick with placards. The Report explains what happened.

'At the lunch hour Mr Sunil Desai and very probably some others arranged with sympathizers, most of them working in the mail-order department, for an afternoon walk-out. It was timed for 3.00 p.m.; about fifty walked out. When the party from inside reached the street, there was shouting and excitement, and an inconclusive parley with management. The strikers decided to march round to Cobbold Road. When they arrived there a violent scene ensued. The strikers were calling upon those who were inside to come out and join them. *Some fiery spirits tried to force an entry and broke some windows.'*

So far, so good, and we might reasonably expect on the basis of this evidence that the Report would state that the dispute was contrived and that Grunwick very properly dismissed those who were intent upon destroying its property.

But the Report draws no such conclusion from the evidence. It does not think Grunwick should have paid much attention to the incident, on the incredible grounds that, 'Although there was some violence, it was short-lived.'

If industrial relations are to be conducted on this basis, then the ordinary rule of law has no place in them. Football supporters, who after the excitement of a match kicked in some shop windows, would not escape punishment in court by pleading, 'Although there was some violence, it was short-lived.'

Here we are not dealing with legal punishment, but only with the universally admitted right of an employer to dismiss an employee for misconduct. Yet according to the Report, an employer should not dismiss for misconduct an employee who commits an act that would be punishable in a court of law.

These are strange standards indeed, and Grunwick rejects them out of hand. We believe the Report, at this point, is seriously in error, illogical in its reasoning, dangerous in its implications, and arguing contrary to custom and practice – not to mention common sense.

Grunwick and trade unions

The attitude of Grunwick to trade unions has been the source of deliberate misrepresentation from the time the dispute began. It is not exaggerating the matter to say, that many within the trade union movement would have taken little account of the dispute, were it not for the constant repetition of the single most important claim of the strikers – that they were dismissed for joining a trade union.

So the findings of the Court of Inquiry on this point are of paramount importance. Though Grunwick believes that the findings do less than justice to the management's attitude, they dispose so effectively of the false claim that workers were dismissed for joining a trade union that the passage is worth quoting.

'Since the company's attitude to unions has been the subject of discussion before us, it is right that we should state our finding explicitly. It was the desire of the directors and top management of the

Company, while professing to accept the right of individual employees to join a trade union, not to recognize a union for collective bargaining purposes; and they have sought up to this day to maintain that policy. They successfully resisted an attempt by the Transport and General Workers Union to secure recognition in 1973, when a few workers (some sixteen, we are told) came out on strike in support of two who had been made redundant. They have sought up to this day to maintain their non-union shop. To this end they have established a works committee, and taken steps to ensure good physical working conditions. Management is 'from the front', in the sense that Managers are always accessible and visible. Money has been spent on maintaining the premises in excellent condition – Chapter Road, in particular, into which the company moved in April 1976, after extensive modernization. We do, however, accept Mr Ward's statement that, if the Company's workforce, or a substantial proportion of it, should evince a wish to be represented by a union, the company would not resist recognition. We also accept his word that the Company recognizes the right of every employee to join a union, if he chooses. Nevertheless the company, we are sure, does all that it can to persuade its employees that they are better placed without a union. There is, we stress, nothing unlawful in the company's attitude towards unionization: but whether in all the circumstances it remains today reasonable is another question – perhaps the fundamental question confronting us.'

Grunwick does less to persuade its workers against joining trade unions than the Report allows. Nevertheless the vital point, that the Company would not resist recognition if the workforce desired it and accepts the right of individual workers to join trade unions, was accepted by the Court of Inquiry.

Where Grunwick might take issue with the Report, if it more clearly understood what was meant, occurs in the phrase, 'but whether in all the circumstances it remains today reasonable is another question – perhaps the fundamental question confronting us'.

In what sense is it less 'reasonable', not to wish to join an association, than to wish to do so? If the law permits an employee not to join a union, why is he unreasonable in exercising that right? And what are the 'circumstances' that 'today' make it unreasonable, or perhaps injudicious, for employees not to join unions and for management to refuse to persuade them to do so?

The passage is too opaque to give any indication of precisely what is meant. Grunwick feels that the underlying implication is that in 1977 trade union power is so great that one is most unwise to resist it too strenuously, or to expect it to observe the circumspection and restraints that are required from everyone else. If that is the meaning, then it is the authentic voice of the Corporate State. Grunwick unhesitatingly rejects it. Trade Unions already enjoy vast legal immunities and in pursuing industrial aims can do more or less as they please. If on top of this, companies are to be deemed unreasonable for exercising what rights they have left and using what little legal protection remains to them, then no society can exist in Britain other than a collectivist one.

The Court of Inquiry and the Grunwick workforce

Nobody has ever denied that the overwhelming majority of Grunwick workers do not wish to be represented by APEX, or to have the strikers reinstated. The Court of Inquiry did not set a precedent by disputing this fact.

Obviously the MORI and Gallup ballots impressed the Inquiry. It referred to MORI as 'an independent body of undoubted integrity'. About the Gallup ballot it was even more explicit.

'But there is no evidence that Mr Ward exerted pressure on his workforce in respect of this poll: and we are satisfied that he was content to allow the situation as it was in July to exert its own pressures upon the opinions of the company's employees.'

Though perhaps expressed in a somewhat cumbersome and even grudging way, this is the clearest possible recognition that the democratic decision of the Grunwick workforce is set firmly against the strikers and their demands.

Whereupon the Grunwick workers' decision disappears from the pages of the Report and is never again mentioned, either directly, or by implication!

Grunwick find this perhaps the most astonishing aspect of the report. Page after page is devoted to the opinions, thoughts and wishes of APEX. Numerous aspects of the dispute are probed, but no reference is made to the Grunwick workforce, nor any comment offered as to how the management is supposed to reconcile them to the presence of a trade union they do not want, and the reinstatement of those who have, to put it mildly, been making their lives unpleasant and their jobs insecure. It is as if, for the Inquiry, the Grunwick workers did not exist.

Grunwick does not believe that this omission is accidental. The workers' opinions are inconvenient, because they do not support the APEX demands. We do not mean that the Inquiry took a conscious decision to ignore them. The fault lies in the whole corporatist attitude

195

of the Inquiry. Workers who do not want to be represented by trade unions must be strange fish indeed. The Inquiry was so convinced that the role of trade unions in industry is wholly beneficent, so concerned to have the APEX strikers back inside Grunwick, that instinctively it shied away from examining the most important piece of evidence in front of it, because the plain meaning of the evidence was to contradict flatly its own intellectual preconceptions.

We believe the Inquiry erred badly on this point. By failing to examine the intensity of the Grunwick workforce's rejection of the strikers' claims it makes nonsense of its principal recommendation. The existing workforce simply would not tolerate the re-employment of the strikers. Not to understand that, is not to understand why the dispute has gone on for so long.

Working conditions at Grunwick

There is no doubt that the report has performed a most valuable public service by disposing of the slanders and libels about working conditions at Grunwick, which were the substance of the APEX case.

The Inquiry quotes from the General Secretary of APEX, Mr Roy Grantham's speech to the 1976 TUC Conference.

'A reactionary employer taking advantage of race and employing workers on disgraceful terms and conditions.'

No more vile charge could be imagined, and in making it Mr Grantham was employing another trade union immunity, the one that frees unions from the legal consequences of acts, when such acts are in furtherance of a trade dispute.

Mr Grantham, as he so frequently explains, is a moderate. Far worse has been alleged by the Grunwick Strike Committee, the Brent Trades Council, the Socialist Workers Party and other participants on the picket line, who are not moderates and who would be insulted if they were so called.

But when the Report is read, what remains of the talk about, 'a nineteenth century sweatshop', 'abominable working conditions', 'workers treated like animals', to quote but a few of the steady stream of lies put out on behalf of the strikers?

The Inquiry says,

'When one turns to working conditions, the same sort of picture emerges. Physical working conditions were reasonably good, and at Chapter Road, save for the mischance with the air conditioning in a hot summer, excellent.'

196

'Reasonably good', all the way to 'excellent'. Hardly the picture painted by APEX and the strikers.

But what of the intolerable oppression of working compulsory overtime in the busy summer months, which the company writes into contracts of employment and which is offset by the very easy pace worked, even during normal hours, throughout the rest of the year?

The Inquiry says, 'Compulsory overtime was at times a burden, but more often was seen as a welcome addition to the wage packet.'

But what about those strikers who were humiliated daily, by having to hold up their hands to go to the lavatory? That never happened either. What did happen is explained by the Inquiry ... 'Asking for permission to go to the lavatory, a requirement which had been imposed at Station Road, Wembley, when the lavatories were *outside the premises occupied by the company*, but was never imposed after the move to Chapter Road.'

Like all other well-run companies, Grunwick wanted to know if any employees left the premises during working hours, but, of course, it has never expected its workers to seek permission to visit lavatories.

That leaves intact very little of the strikers' case. As indeed the Inquiry concedes, though it has an explanation. It says, speaking of the strikers' attitudes: 'While it remains difficult to define with precision what the grievances were, the evidence leaves us in no doubt of the fact that they were felt. Of course, it does not follow that because they were felt they were justified.'

Quite so. Grunwick would like to ask, whoever heard of a dispute of this length, pursued with this degree of violence, accompanied by so much anti-management propaganda, of which it could be said, 'it remains difficult to define with precision what the grievances were'?

The Inquiry and the Brent Trades Council

An answer to the question posed in the last paragraph might have been forthcoming, if the Inquiry had looked more closely at the composition, and role in the dispute played by the Brent Trades Council.

The Inquiry agrees that Mr Jack Dromey, the Secretary of the Brent Trades Council, 'provided substantial support for the strike and exercised great influence upon the strikers, all of whom were ill-acquainted with the conduct of industrial relations in Britain ...' The point unfortunately is pursued no further.

Grunwick wishes to predict, that much more will be heard of Mr Jack Dromey, whose views as expressed to the Court of Inquiry on the

197

issues of our day and age will become increasingly apparent. It will be of particular interest to see how Mr Dromey's relations with APEX and the TUC develop.

Grunwick and grievances

Where Grunwick is disposed to accept a measure of criticism contained in the Report is in respect of its grievance procedure.

The Inquiry says, 'If there be no adequate ways and means of handling grievances even fanciful ones can pose serious industrial problems.'

The Inquiry is stating a general proposition and not accusing Grunwick of having no means of dealing with grievances. Nevertheless, it is critical of the procedures that existed at the time the dispute began.

Grunwick will not plead all the difficulties that it has encountered in this sphere. It accepts that there was room for improvement in its grievance procedure. Everything has been done to make certain that no similar complaint can be made in the future.

Grunwick does not for a moment believe that any employee was unjustly treated, but has changed its procedure so that even the suspicion that this might be so has been obviated. We accept that in industrial relations the 'fanciful' element can play a part.

Grunwick wishes to have a bargaining relationship with its workers that accepts them as industrial partners in a productive enterprise. Perhaps the courage and loyalty of the Grunwick workforce will be accepted as evidence that this relationship is well-understood on the shop-floor.

Grunwick and the Court of Inquiry's recommendations

As will be apparent from the foregoing, Grunwick does not believe that the recommendations of the Inquiry follow from the evidence that the Inquiry accepted.

It might have been better if the Inquiry had pursued its original intention and made no reference to admitted trade union illegalities. The censure of the Inquiry upon trade unions for law-breaking is couched in such terms as to make probable a repetition of the offence, and gives no hope to those who would wish to see official bodies at least attempt to differentiate between those who break the law and those who are at pains to observe it.

Where possible Grunwick will meet the recommendations of the

Inquiry; but regrettably the eccentric nature of the Report, its heavily corporatist prejudices, its equation of opposites, and its inability to pronounce authoritatively, on matters of principle that cannot be pushed aside in the interests of peace at any price, make the extent to which Grunwick can bind itself, severely limited.

Grunwick will accept the second of the three recommendations set forth on page 23 of the Report. As the Company explained to the Inquiry it has always been prepared to allow any employee who wishes it, to have a trade union bargain on his or her behalf. We have no hesitation in re-affirming this declaration and thus complying with recommendation (2).

Recommendation (3) is not a recommendation at all, but merely a comment upon the role of trade unions as seen by the Inquiry. We have made our views clear on this matter.

Grunwick will recognize APEX as having the right to bargain for such members of the existing workforce as wish to join it, if the House of Lords overturns the judgement of the Court of Appeal.

Recommendation (1) Grunwick rejects in its entirety. Never under any circumstances will the company reinstate those who were very properly dismissed. The suggestion is completely impracticable, as the existing Grunwick workforce would never accept it. Additionally, Grunwick believes that reinstatement would be a surrender to rampant illegality, brute force, and the coercive power of a mighty vested interest that seeks not to reason, but to compel.

The suggestion that *ex gratia* payments be made to strikers upon recommendations of a mediator confirms Grunwick's impression, derived from earlier sections of the Report, that the Court of Inquiry does not understand the provisions of the Employment Protection Act, nor is it fully cognisant of the way industrial tribunals determine cases. Grunwick rejects any such suggestion of payments to those who by their own actions terminated their employment.

The issue of determining supposed vacancies therefore does not arise. Grunwick has acted within the law, both in letter and spirit. It will not abandon its legal rights and is shocked that it should be asked to do so.

If, by illegal action, the company is forced out of business, it will accept its fate, in the hope that such a fate will arouse public opinion to demand better protection from the authorities for those who legally go about their business. Grunwick, if it is ruined by illegal coercion, will generously recompense its loyal workforce and go into liquidation. But the Company believes it will survive and prosper. If it does not, it will bear that, rather than submit and give another hostage to an iniquitous tyranny.

More About Penguins
and Pelicans

A Pelican Book

The New Unionism:
The Case for Workers' Control

Ken Coates and Tony Topham

At a time of severe crisis in the Labour Movement, there has
never been a greater need for rethinking about the aims and
methods of socialism. Ken Coates and Tony Topham, who 'have
been tireless in their arguments within the Labour Movement
about its future', here set out proposals for a new unionism to
replace the present bureaucratic structures.

In presenting the case for full self-management as the only way
of attaining a rational and humane society, the authors deal with
both the opportunities and the dangers, with genuine workers'
control and with illusory schemes of 'participation'.

As Hugh Scanlon said in *Labour Weekly*, *The New Unionism* will
'be welcomed by trade unionists and labour activists . . . The
continued march of the Movement . . . will be aided by this book.
The ferment of ideas contained in it mirrors the ferment of
activity in the Movement itself. It can be warmly recommended.'

A Pelican Book

The Origins of Modern Leftism

Richard Gombin

'All revolutions up to now have been failures. The revolution has to be reinvented.'

Since 1917 the left has been dominated by Marxism–Leninism. Critiques from the right have been frequent, but more seriously damaging has been the association of the left with the ideology of Stalin and of State capitalism. But in recent years a new kind of leftism has found its feet.

Modern leftism uses Marxist analysis to achieve a rigorous critique of Marxism–Leninism; regards Marx as the theoretician of the *bourgeois* revolution; acknowledges Dada and Surrealism as crucial influences; denies absolutely any revolutionary ideology; and bids fair to occupy the vacuum left in the revolutionary tradition by the failure of official communism.

Richard Gombin, drawing largely on the French experience, clarifies the genesis, thought and influence of modern leftism. Tracing its history from the early critiques of the USSR, and examining the influence of such writers as Lukács and Lefebvre, he provides a coherent exposition of the radical alternative to Marxism–Leninism.

A Penguin Special

Civil Liberty: The NCCL Guide

Anna Coote and Lawrence Grant

Revised Edition

No constitution or charter protects British rights. At the mercy of any piece of hasty or prejudiced legislation, they must be upheld in every generation.

Do you possess the 'eternal vigilance' required to safeguard liberty? Do you know, for instance, what your rights are if you are arrested or need legal aid; if you are discriminated against or evicted; if you want to cancel a hire purchase agreement or make a complaint against your doctor; if you are getting a divorce or adopting a baby; if you hold a public meeting or go on strike?

If you are unsure, this Penguin Special will supply the answers. You will find detailed here all those questions of liberty, justice and human rights about which most men in the street are ignorant or, at best, doubtful. In effect this well ordered and useful guide distils the long experience of the National Council for Civil Liberties in standing up (both politically and through case-work) for 'us' against 'them'.

A Pelican Book

The Technology of Political Control

Carol Ackroyd, Karen Margolis,
Jonathan Rosenhead, Tim Shallice

As the incidence of political dissent increases, the Army and police are preparing to undertake a more active role in dealing with civil unrest. The security forces are becoming more concerned with defending the state against attacks from within rather than from outside. And the technology for this is being developed – new forms of riot control, sophisticated techniques of interrogation, surveillance and civilian intelligence – while the military and civilian authorities are learning to cooperate more closely in anticipation of widespread disorder.

At the same time the law is changing. The flexibility of the Common Law is being manipulated and combined with piecemeal legislation like the Prevention of Terrorism Act in order to provide the legal basis for the 'Strong State' which is building.

The authors of this book explain the nature and extent of the technological and political changes which are taking place. They have written a chilling book on what is certainly the central political question of our time.

A Penguin Special

Civil Liberties in Britain

Barry Cox

Britain is one of the freest countries in the world; but the rights which many of us take for granted are not protected by charter and their maintenance needs constant vigilance; The 1930s were a particularly dangerous time when governments attempted to regain powers which they had had during the First World War. But the 1970s may be an even more dangerous decade. As more people become aware of their rights and are prepared to assert them, there will be attempts to restrict them.

Civil Liberties in Britain is a history of the civil rights movement, of how the basic rights – of association, assembly, expression and movement – have been threatened and fought over for the past fifty years; and a survey of the areas in which personal freedoms are open to abuse – the courts, the police, legislation, industry and the armed services.

Barry Cox concludes that while there have been some changes for the better since 1934, when the National Council for Civil Liberties was founded, we have no reason for complacency.

A Pelican Book

Class in a Capitalist Society:
A Study of Contemporary Britain
John Westergaard and Henrietta Resler

The notion that class inequality has been steadily diminishing is a myth. In Britain, as in other western capitalist countries, class structures and therefore class divisions are both deeply rooted and pervasive. In other words, and contrary to popular pretence, 'class' is alive and well and flourishing in contemporary society.

The theme of this book, therefore, is class inequality: its nature and extent today; its roots; the conflicts and tensions to which it gives rise, both overt and latent; the prospects of change – radical and revolutionary, or reactionary and repressive – to which recent shifts in the character and tempo of conflict may point. The authors draw on evidence which relates largely to Britain, but the focus is not peculiarly British. Britain is used as a case study – to illustrate and document in detail features which, so the authors argue, are common to and inherent in contemporary capitalism throughout the western world.

The authors' perspective is Marxist, but this is not another restatement of Marxist theory in abstract and general terms. It is an attempt to anchor a Marxist analysis and interpretation of class in empirical fact; and at the same time to dispel the clouds of myth and mystification with which, in the authors' view, much conventional sociological commentary has surrounded the subject.